The Snarktastic Guide to College Success

edited by

Sandra Mizumoto Posey
Teague von Bohlen

PEARSON

Boston • Columbus • Indianapolis • New York • San Francisco • Upper Saddle River
Amsterdam • Cape Town • Dubai • London • Madrid • Milan • Munich • Paris • Montréal • Toronto
Delhi • Mexico City • São Paulo • Sydney • Hong Kong • Seoul • Singapore • Taipei • Tokyo

Editor in Chief: Jodi McPherson
Acquisitions Editor: Katie Mahan
Development Editor: Elana Dolberg
Editorial Assistant: Erin Carreiro
Senior Managing Editor: Karen Wernholm
Executive Marketing Manager: Amy Judd
Marketing Assistant: Megan Zuccarini
Production Project Manager: Mary Sanger
Procurement Specialist: Dennis Para
Image Manager: Rachel Youdelman
Project Manager, Image Rights and Permissions: Diahanne Lucas
Design and Project Coordination: Electronic Publishing Services Inc., NYC
Composition: Aptara, Inc.
Creative Director, Cover: Jayne Conte
Cover Design: John Christiana

Image Credits: Pages 1, 31, 67, 89, 109: Andrewgenn/Fotolia

Library of Congress Cataloging-in-Publication Data

Posey, Sandra Mizumoto.
The snarktastic guide to college success/Sandra Mizumoto Posey, Metropolitan State University, Teague von Bohlen, University of Colorado Denver. — First edition.
pages cm
Includes bibliographical references.
ISBN 0-321-94732-0
1. College student orientation. 2. Study skills. I. Bohlen, Teague. II. Title.
LB2343.3.P67 2014
378.1'98—dc23 2013045036

10 9 8 7—V092—18 17 16

PEARSON

ISBN-10: 0-321-94732-0
ISBN-13: 978-0-321-94732-1

To our daughters,
Jezebel, Teagan, and Tamsen,
that they might succeed
where we stumbled.

About the Editors

Sandra Mizumoto Posey works to bring out the best in every student. Why? Because once upon a time, she was a failing student and high school dropout. Eventually she turned it all around and went on to graduate from Cal State Long Beach with honors, then earned her master's degree and Ph.D. in folklore from UCLA. Yes, she knows that is the most useless degree you can possibly get. As her friend's mom once said, "Good school, bad major." Still, it has served her well. She's the director of Learning Communities and First Year Success at Metropolitan State University of Denver, where she is also an associate professor of women's studies. Prior to that, she was associate professor of interdisciplinary general education and interim director of the Center for Community Service-Learning at California State Polytechnic University Pomona. There she earned tenure, something she is now so fond of that she takes it wherever she goes, like her yorkie. She has taught at the college level for over a dozen years, mostly to freshmen, a term she can't use because it's too gender biased. After all, she is a women's studies professor. She prefers "first-year student," even though it doesn't roll off the tongue. When things do roll off the tongue, she's actually pretty funny. Don't tell her I said so. Feminists are scary.

Teague von Bohlen enjoys sharing the title "professor" with his colleagues Plum, Dumbledore, Xavier, and Flutesnoot. He's won several awards for his teaching: several student-service prizes from his Creative Writing M.F.A. alma mater, Arizona State University, and two faculty excellence in teaching awards from the University of Colorado Denver, where he currently teaches fiction and serves as primary advisor to the student newspaper *The Advocate*. He's free-lanced (which too many people think he actually does for free) for magazines such as *Westword* and *Village Voice Media*, serving as everything from pop-culture critic to political commentator to humorist. (The humor part is, to be fair, a matter of opinion.) His first novel, *The Pull of the Earth,* won the Colorado Book Award for Fiction in 2007. His short fiction has been seen in magazines and journals, most recently *South Dakota Review, Hawaii Pacific Review, Superstition Review, Waccamaw Review,* and many other publications that end with the word *Review.* He's currently working on a collection of flash fiction and a second novel, mainly because he likes the irony of writing both very long things and very short things at the same time. He's very tall, loves comic books, and is extremely proud to have never seen an episode of *Jersey Shore.*

Table of Contents

Contributors

College Staff, Administrators, and Faculty

Leslie Bailey
Metropolitan State University of Denver
Former Program Assistant, Institute of Women's Studies and Services

Bridgette Coble, Ph.D.
Metropolitan State University of Denver
Director, Office of Career Services

Kevin Haworth, M.F.A.
Ohio University Honors Tutorial College
Assistant Professor

Randy Hyman, Ph.D.
Metropolitan State University of Denver
Associate Vice President of Student Success

Heather Joseph-Witham, Ph.D.
Otis College of Art and Design
Associate Professor, Liberal Arts and Sciences

John A. Lanning, Ph.D.
University of Colorado, Denver
Professor, Chemistry
Assistant Vice Chancellor for Undergraduate Experiences

Antone Minard, Ph.D.
University of British Columbia/Simon Fraser University

Patricia Colleen Murphy, M.F.A.
Arizona State University
Senior Lecturer

Nancy Williams Parks, M.A.
Pierpont Community and Technical College, West Virginia
Associate Professor
Director of Testing, Assessment, and Advising

Teshia Young Roby, Ph.D., M.B.A.
California State Polytechnic University, Pomona
Associate Professor, College of Education and Integrative Studies

Nathan Rudibaugh
University of Denver
Senior Financial Aid Advisor

Victoria Simmons, Ph.D.
Design Institute of San Diego

Eileen V. Wallis, Ph.D.
California State Polytechnic University, Pomona
Associate Professor, History

Students

Daniel Alvarez
Mindy Bezdek
Megan Fowler
Gellilla Gebre-Michael
Thorin Klosowski
Jef Otte
Tasha Ringo
Bryan Smith
Adam Steininger

Acknowledgments

Thanks to our students, past and present, good and bad, for inspiring us to write and edit this snarky volume. Thanks to our moms, dads, kids, bosses, colleagues, partners, friends, dogs, cats, and other distractions for driving us to be concise. Thanks to our contributors for not writing like academics. And thanks especially to the staff at Pearson (Jodi McPherson, Katie Mahan, Erin Carreiro, Amy Judd, Mary Sanger, Louis Hickman, Brian Kracke, Alexandra Diskin, Marcia Flynn, and Elana Dolberg) and Robert E. Leon at Electronic Publishing Services for being as snarky as we are by believing in this project in the first place. Y'all are awesome.

foreword

Forewarned

Sandra Mizumoto Posey and Teague von Bohlen

Be prepared: College is different from the rest of your life, before and after, in so many ways. What you'll be expected to do and say, and how you'll be expected to say it, is unique to this particular world, rooted as it is in medieval traditions and customs. Just take a look at the Dungeons & Dragons-like regalia professors wear to every graduation and you'll know that this is a world with its own bizarre and opaque set of rules. But they're rules the professors expect you to know coming in—we hear it every day in the choruses of complaints about how students come to college "underprepared." Every generation of professors has made the same complaint.

But why another book on student success? There are a lot of them out there, filled with all sorts of useful information—study skills, test-taking, time and fiscal management, social acclimation, even paper decimation. Yes, a lot of trees have met their deaths over these books, for what one hopes is a good cause: your success in, and hopefully eventually out of, college.

The thing is, most of these books aren't all that fun to read. The information is there, but if you're having issues with study skills to begin with, why would a textbook on study skills help you? The fact of the matter is, most of us don't like reading textbooks. Really. Even college professors. (That, by the way, was an incomplete sentence. Don't use them in college.) We don't like reading textbooks *or* writing them. This, on the other hand, is a book for students and professors alike: something we enjoyed writing and something we hope you'll enjoy reading. We've even made all the selections short. After all, who doesn't read while sitting on the toilet? What? You don't? OK, forget we mentioned it. No, we don't do it either. That's gross. Shut up.

The essays in this book come from a variety of different perspectives—professors, students, graduates, college staff, and administrators. All of them have something useful to share. We know this because we hear all their conversations about you after you leave the room—all the complaints about what you did wrong that you could have done right. Stuff that you didn't even know you were supposed to do because no one told you to your face. So here they are, face, the facts.

We all learn through stumbling around and making mistakes, and this book may help you to avoid a few of those. Our advice is practical. We won't just tell you how to study; we'll tell you other things you need to know in order to make college (and life thereafter) as successful as possible.

What Is Snarktastic?

We are! Snarktastic is a combination of (1) "snarky," the somewhat tongue-in-cheek, even sarcastic, use of humor to ironically reveal truth, and (2) "fantastic." *Tastic* is a great suffix, indicating something that transcends itself to enter into the realm of the sublime. No, we're not making these up. OK, maybe we are. The folklorist among us (that's me, Sandra) will tell you that words emerge out of popular speech all the time. Just because it's not in a dictionary today doesn't mean it won't appear there tomorrow. Should you therefore make up words when you are writing your paper for freshman composition? The English professor among us (that's me, Teague, pronounced, against all odds, like the color "beige") will tell you "No." Your class assignment is simply not the place for coining a new word. The weirdos in those medieval Dungeons & Dragons robes (your professors) will fail you for it. We can be just that arbitrary. But there are ways to win us over, and those are just the sort of secrets we'll share with you along the snarktastic way.

See, part of being in college is learning "academic discourse"—that's academese for the way we speak and write in an academic setting. Here's your first secret: There's nothing inherently practical or universal to the way you learned to write and compose an essay in high school; nor is there anything inherently practical or universal to the way you will learn to write in college. What you will learn is the appropriate language for a particular setting. That doesn't mean you're learning useless skills, only that you are broadening your toolset. If you have a house to build and all you have is a hammer, you'll only get so far. If you've also got nails, screws, and maybe even a Sawzall, you'll get further. Look at all the impractical and practical things you'll learn in college as the power tools of life.

This book is part of that. If college had an instruction manual, it'd look like those other college success guides. But who really reads the instruction manual before using a power tool?

You do? Good for you. Most of us don't.

If, on the other hand, college had a funny YouTube video of someone using and misusing power tools, it'd look a lot like this book. Yes, we know a book isn't a YouTube video. If you want a YouTube video, go to YouTube. If you want bathroom reading, come to us. We are the power tools of bathroom reading.

Wait. What does that even mean?

To be honest, we don't know. Let that be a lesson to you: Don't mix your metaphors. See, there are all sorts of secrets to be had in here. Take a seat, wherever that seat may be, and start reading. We promise to be funny and we promise to be honest. We promise, even when we're a bit harsh, that we're all rooting for you to graduate. We really are. After all, we were once where you are. We'll share what we know about how to get through college, through trouble, and even through life.

section one

Before Class

Nancy Williams Parks

1. Picking Your College and Picking Your Battles

Advice from a Professor and Director of Advising...

There are good reasons and bad reasons to pick a college, pick a roommate, and pick your future. Let's start with some of the bad reasons.

First, don't attend a particular college just because your boyfriend or girlfriend is going there. That sounds romantic now, but you'll soon realize how ridiculous that is. There are great people and good-looking guys and girls everywhere you go. Do you really want to be stuck with your high school sweetheart the rest of your life? Yes? Then you're really in love and you'll wait for each other if you want to attend separate schools. No? Then now's the time to play the *"It's not you, it's me"* card.

On the same note, think twice before you room with a best friend. Ask yourself, "*What do I want more—having a roommate I already know well or keeping my best friend as my best friend?*" There's no guarantee that same person will still be both by the end of your first semester. You can still hang out with each other—and more importantly, still want to—even if you aren't rooming together. And your moms can always return the matching shams and comforters.

So toss out these security blankets; you don't need them. Even if you go away to college and find yourself absolutely miserable there, know that if you can make it through the first two weeks without packing up and going home (physically, or mentally "checking out"), you will be much more likely to stick it out the entire semester. Likewise, many students report that a college they didn't like their first semester is one they grew to love when they returned after Christmas break. Think about all the reasons you decided to attend that particular school and focus on those points. You may get homesick—but that issue may remedy itself once you're home for a while and get really sick of *that.*

Once you have your living conditions chosen, the next step is to learn how to wake up. And the way adults do that (yes, you're one of us now) is this: on time, on your own. You're going to have morning classes, and this is a life skill you'll desperately need from here forward. Try moving your phone from underneath your pillow and put it on the opposite side of your room at night. And set it to actually ring, not just vibrate. If you can't wake yourself up on your first day of college, you're going to have a rough semester. If you're thinking to yourself, "No big deal . . . I'll still be living at home and my mom will wake me up," well, then shame on you.

See, college is the time to learn how to take responsibility for yourself. You owe yourself this. And if you're the oldest kid in your family, you especially don't want to mess this up for your younger brothers and sisters. If you go away to college and screw up, your parents are going to think twice before investing so much time and money in their other kids. If you're the youngest in your family, don't take advantage of the fact that your parents are probably just really tired by now and have stopped paying much attention. Don't make them regret having had you—or don't make them say that out loud, anyway.

See, college is the time to learn how to take responsibility for yourself.

Speaking of parents—college isn't the best time to become one. Remember, regardless of the current fertility problems the celebrities of the moment might be having, it is very easy to get pregnant. **Very easy.** Especially when you're not planning on it. Don't assume the other person is taking care of it. Even if he or she says, *"I've got it taken care of,"* translate that as *"Yeah, yeah, let's just get on with it."* Visit your student health center on an as-needed basis—before you run out of whatever you need to prevent this. This statement, by the way, is in no way intended to encourage anyone to become sexually active if they're not, but to be a reminder that "19 and Pregnant" often looks just like "16 and Pregnant."

But it's not just the major life events that can mess up your college career; it's the little things that make a difference too. For example, please do not wear pajamas to class. They are not "flannel pants;" they're pajama bottoms. Appearances sometimes really **are** everything. Give your professors the appearance, at least, that you care enough about attending class that you'll get dressed.

So what now? You've got it all pulled together. Except for that day when you don't. We all get colds. If you have a cold, don't try to skip three days of class and call it the flu. If you have a hangover, don't try to pass it off as a "stomach virus" or "food poisoning." Force yourself to wake up and work through it: that's the best deterrent from getting another one.

Timeliness goes for other things too: observe office hours and schedule appointments whenever possible. If office hours are posted as 10 a.m.–noon, that means you need to be there *before* noon, not *at* noon. If you have an appointment, be on time or just a couple minutes early: showing up 20 minutes before your scheduled time can be as rude as showing up late. College faculty and staff don't schedule the same way the cable guys do.

College is an experience of self-discovery, one of the ways you'll work to define who you are and what your life path will be. Make sure your first steps on that journey will be ones you can be proud of.

Randy Hyman

2. Cutting the Academic Umbilical Cord

Preparing Your Parents for Your College Experience

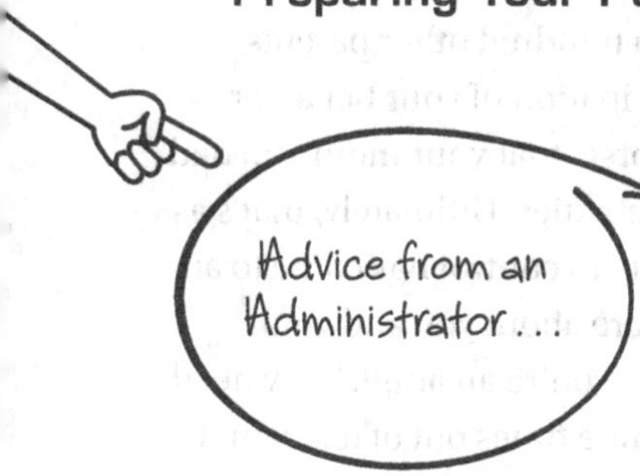
Advice from an Administrator . . .

Most of you, if pressed, would prefer your parents not learn very much about what you might be up to at college. However . . .

Be aware that many colleges not only encourage but often require parents to attend an orientation program. Such programs, designed specifically for them, are usually scheduled concurrent with your own orientation visit to campus.

It's probably a good idea to invite your parents to participate . . . far better that they learn about the many challenges you'll face as a college student from someone on the campus who understands. Of course, many such parent ambassadors "sugar coat" the real issues, plying your mom and dad with all sorts of semi-useless drivel about studying 30 hours a week, attending class, being courteous to your roommate, going to the campus dining hall on a regular basis, avoiding credit cards, etc. However, especially savvy campus officials tell your folks the truth . . . about the importance of practicing safe sex; about the eating disorder that manifests itself in your first semester, about the parking tickets you accumulate and fail to pay, resulting in your car being impounded; about the midterm deficiency notices that you receive that they don't get copies of because of the federal law that protects your privacy.

Parents can get pretty riled up when confronted with the "real story" of your potential college experience. Most have never thought that they won't have access to your grades, even though they are paying the bills. It never occurred to them that the federal laws, designed to protect your privacy, would deprive them of information they consider crucial to their support of your college experience. They never considered that, if they want to know something, about you, they will have to ASK YOU!

Many will resort to denial, publicly declaring in front of hundreds of other parents that "my son would never be arrested with a blood alcohol level of 1.5." Or the typical, "my daughter was always on the honor roll and will certainly make the dean's list in college," not considering for a moment that she will likely find herself in classes filled with high school valedictorians.

It's in settings like this, in a room with at least a hundred other parents, chewing their respective upper lips in anxious anticipation of your behavior provoking your prompt removal from college, or worse, that your mom and dad face the reality they are powerless to control your activities. Ultimately, that's as it should be. Parents must understand that their duty to control has come to an end. It's now time for them to accept their duty to care about you and your success, recognizing that, whether they like it or not, you're an adult. They need to realize if they learn to treat you as an adult, that nine times out of ten, you'll respond as one.

How can this happen . . . this evolution in the parent-child relationship? Lots of "C" words come to mind. You've already been exposed to four . . . challenge, control, care, credit card . . . or is that five? There are many more, including contraception, condoms, choices, consequences, change, curriculum, cheating, and communicate. Each of them has the potential to influence the evolving relationship with your parents.

How can this happen . . .
this evolution in the
parent-child relationship?

You know them best. You realize their fears and their anxieties. You are ideally prepared to help your parents understand how they can support you in your efforts to grow and develop as a young adult. If your college's parent advisor doesn't speak about the real issues, then you must. It's your responsibility to clarify ground rules and expectations about how you wish to interact with them. Realize that they too probably expect certain things of you, especially if they are providing any significant financial support for your education.

Sit down for a frank conversation with them before you leave home. Speak openly and honestly about all things that might present unique challenges, whether academic or otherwise. Prepare an agenda in advance so that you don't overlook anything important that needs your collective consideration. Tell them you trust they will give you time, space, and distance. Let them know they can trust you to make good life decisions. Agree to consult (talk on the phone, visit) regularly but not constantly.

Parents can make or break your college adventure. If you're smart, you'll communicate, collaborate, and commiserate at the appropriate times. Adopting these three behaviors into this new relationship with your parents will help ensure they will be your allies, rather than your adversaries in this journey we call the college experience.

3. Be Good to the Gatekeeper

Please Don't Call Us Secretaries

Advice from a Department Coordinator . . .

We're not secretaries. We're department coordinators. There's a difference, and it goes beyond job descriptions.

We're the people you rely on for the information you need to not only go to school, but to do it in such a way that you'll actually graduate. We're the gatekeepers of your education. We may not teach, but we know exactly how things work outside the classroom—which is just as vital for you to know in order to get that diploma.

So, before seeking help from your department coordinator, you should do one thing: *know what you know, and know what you don't know*. In other words, the more clearly and specifically you communicate your needs or questions, the greater the chances of someone being able to accurately and pleasantly answer your question or help you. Put yet another way, sign up for Communication 101 in your first semester.

A common phrase that department coordinators often hear from students (OK, to be honest, sometimes from faculty) is "I don't know where my class is." Or "Where is my class?" This phrase is like arriving at a new city and asking a stranger on the street if they can tell you where "the store is." What store? Who are you again, and what exactly are you looking for? They might be able to help if they knew the name of the store you were looking for, or what that store sold, or had some idea of the street names or intersection to which you need direction. In not phrasing your question thoughtfully or thoroughly, you greatly increase the chances of a short and aggravated response from the person from whom you seek help, unless, of course, you catch them on a really good day. (Hey, it's possible.)

Instead, try one of the following phrases:

Slightly Better: "Can you tell me where the classroom is located for English 101?"

Golden: "I'm registered for English 101, section 8, with Professor X. I'm a new student, and I'm not sure how to figure out where the class meets. Do you have the time to help me, so I can know how to find this information myself next time?"

Sure, it might take you a little longer to pose the question, but better that than eat up the time of an already overwhelmed and overburdened department coordinator who has to field and decipher how to answer dozens of the exact same questions all day long. Phrasing a question thoughtfully and articulately demonstrates: (1) that the answer, simple as it may be, will not be lost on the student but rather comprehended, and (2) your willingness to learn how to find the answer on your own in the future. After all, the old "teach a man to fish" idiom is pretty perfect for the educational arena.

Another important aspect to that "golden" example is that it shows some respect for our time. We're swamped most of the time, to be honest, because there's a lot of moving parts in making sure a department runs smoothly, both for the faculty and the students. But we're probably most busy right at the times when you're most likely to have pressing questions—at the beginning of the term and at the end. Respecting the time of your department coordinators is always a good idea—but especially at those times when everyone is stressed out. A little kindness goes a long way.

This kindness extends to other areas too. Sometimes, for example, you don't want to ask a question in person, but rather over the phone or via email. When calling a department coordinator, you want to always leave your name, phone number, and a short (short!) message about what you're calling about, remembering to speak slowly and clearly. This greatly increases your chances of getting a return call. As for email—well, treating it more like the business

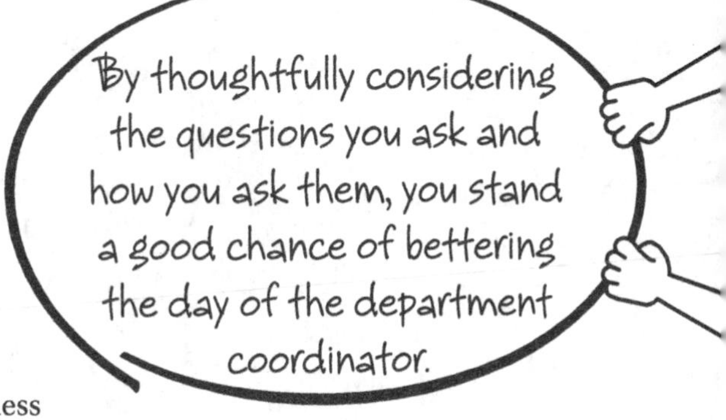
By thoughtfully considering the questions you ask and how you ask them, you stand a good chance of bettering the day of the department coordinator.

correspondence that it is will go a long way toward making it understandable and effective. Remember: you're not texting your BFF.

By thoughtfully considering the questions you ask and how you ask them, you stand a good chance of bettering the day of the department coordinator. Think of it as departmental karma—what goes around, comes around. At some point in your education, you'll probably need us for something. You want us to remember your responsibility and respect when you ask that favor. Just don't call us secretaries, and you're off to a good start.

Eileen V. Wallis

4. Beyond the Chili Pepper

Scheduling Classes and Picking Your Professors

Advice from a Professor . . .

Congratulations! If you're reading this, you've probably already successfully completed Step 1: Get into College. Now comes Step 2: Find Some Classes.

Before you sit down in front of that computer to register, you need a plan. Otherwise it will be 2 a.m. on the first day of classes, and there you'll be: hopped up on venti lattes, still without any classes on your schedule, and frantically scrolling through ratemyprofessors.com trying to decipher their chili pepper–based ratings system.

Yeah, you read that right. Chili peppers. They rate professors with chili peppers. For hotness.

But never fear. With some basic knowledge and a few more food-based metaphors, you'll be ready to sign up for that perfect class schedule. One that will meet your academic needs, leave you (some) time for a personal life, and still get you to graduation.

Think of your education as a visit to your local ice cream shop. (No, really. Work with me here for a second.) In high school you had perhaps three flavors of ice cream to choose from: vanilla, chocolate, and strawberry. There might have been the occasional exotic flavor, the intellectual equivalent of rum raisin. But your choices were still limited, and your education was pretty similar to that of millions of young people around the country. State and federal education codes, after all, prioritize vanilla and chocolate learning over Chubby Hubby.

But college? Oh boy, college! Vanilla and chocolate are still there, of course, but so are dozens of mix-ins, tasty things you can add to customize your education to your own tastes. And we, your faculty and administrators, will put very few limits on those mix-ins. Want to add crushed cookies to your education? Go for it. Heck, want to add bacon and wasabi paste? Knock yourself out.

So how do you, the student, create a tasty education with the right mixture of classes? How do you make an educational rocky road instead of some Frankenmixture that will leave you will a stomach ache and an empty wallet? Simple. You study your options, and you plan ahead.

Whether you're an incoming freshman, a transfer from another institution, or a returning student, the first thing to find out is what the basic "vanilla" education looks like at your university. Every institution has these sets of classes. They're often called simply "general education," (abbreviated to GE) or "core" classes. These classes are designed to give you as broad an education as possible, no matter what you are majoring in. Students across the campus will all need to satisfy the same GE requirements.

You, and every student around you, will complain mightily about GE requirements. Get over it. Accept the fact you will have to take some classes you don't want to take. It's part of the learning experience. We want you to graduate as a well-rounded human being. And if that means making you sit through a philosophy class, we are totally crazy enough to do that.

Plan ahead for how you are going to satisfy all those GE requirements. Familiarize yourself with GE and decide which courses you want to take when and in what order. A really smart student (and you're reading this book, so you must be one of those, right?) will sketch out a rough plan for every semester before he or she graduates, as well as an overall super-structure that keeps an eye on the requirements for (eventual) graduation. This approach makes a little procrastination acceptable. Your plan may put off that music appreciation class you've been dreading until your very last semester. We're cool with that. Just remember that not all classes will be offered when you want them. Stay flexible.

What mix of classes "tastes" the best? That depends on you. Personally I never recommend a student take only GE courses during a given semester. Slogging through three or four classes you're not happy to be in all at once can be soul crushing. After all, you have a major with its own course requirements to satisfy—the yummy stuff you actually came here to study. One effective approach is to take one or two of GE courses (your vanilla base) at a time, along with one or two courses from your major (the mix-ins.)

What mix of classes "tastes" the best?

So now you're in line, looking for a nice base of ice cream and a few tasty toppings. But imagine that this will be the first time you've ever eaten ice cream. How do you choose between vanilla and chocolate? Between sprinkles and nuts?

The same conundrum faces students when choosing courses and professors. In high school, if you took a biology class it was a biology class. In college, there might be ten different biology classes that satisfy the same requirement. How do you choose between courses with titles like "Decomposition and You" or "Meet the Protists"? Here again, research comes in handy. Check out your college's course catalog. There should be a longer description of each course, including topics covered. It may also give the number of hours of study expected, both inside and outside the classroom.

Most importantly, get out there and talk to people. Students are usually pretty open about discussing positive and negative experiences they've had with classes and professors. If you like, you can also check one of the professor ratings sites already mentioned. There are several out there: find the one most people at your school use. Ignore both the most glowing review of a class or faculty member ("He was the most brilliant professor ever in the history of the universe!") and the most negative one ("All who look upon this professor shall despair!"). Focus on the middle chunk of reviews to help you make a decision.

Most importantly, get out there and talk to people.

Above all, take recommendations with a grain of salt. Keep in mind that a class you might enjoy, like that custom ice cream flavor, is not necessarily one others will enjoy, and vice versa.

Now, how about some mocha chili swirl to go?

Teague von Bohlen

5. Oh, the Humanities!

A Defense of the Well-Rounded Education

Advice from a Professor . . .

You may not think that someone could write an apt comparison between giving props to the beleaguered humanities and the Hindenburg disaster . . . but you'd be wrong. Oh, so very wrong.

Because let's face it: Both are sort of disasters.

Clearly, they're disasters in different ways. The Hindenburg killed 36 people back in 1937. The humanities have only ruined some GPAs here and there (mostly for you business majors out there who didn't think you needed it). But more importantly, this field has been more and more pushed to the margins of educational life by degree programs that don't appreciate what its subjects have to offer. And those degree programs don't appreciate it because their students tend not to either.

(So far, this doesn't sound like much a defense, does it? Wait for it.)

To understand why the humanities are important, first we'll need to be specific about what subjects the field of humanities includes. It's a big group: literature; the visual and dramatic arts; music; philosophy; languages; history; and something called classics, which more or less means the study of ancient cultures. On one hand, this is stuff that everyone recognizes would be sort of cool to know—you know, the stuff that professors with a capital *P* can recite from memory at cocktail parties to impress everyone with their smarty-pants-ness. On the other hand, what if you're not a professor, and you don't go to cocktail parties much, and you just want to move on to an MBA or to medical or law school and make some cash to pay off all those student loans? It seems like it's eminently skippable.

But it's important to remember that the humanities were at one time part of the requisite foundation of any higher education. College was originally—and arguably still should be—more than just career training. Originally, it was study for study's sake. In order to be an effective member of society, in order to lead a good civic life, it was assumed that a person would know how to speak another language; know something about literature, about making an effective argument, or about other cultures; or understand any of the arts. This was deemed important for being . . . well, a person. It's what being an educated person meant. And should still mean.

One of the goals of the university experience was to make its graduates more "well-rounded." It's why high school extracurriculars like the yearbook committee or the French club make any difference at all in the decision as to whether you get that acceptance letter from your dream college. Because "well-rounded" (even though it makes you sound like we're fattening you up) is still a good thing. It still means that you know more than the stuff you'll have to know in order to become an accountant or a nurse or a teacher or an architect. It means that you have more to offer the world at large than just the minimum you'll need to get by.

This is the value of the humanities: Knowing them makes you a better human being, a more complete participant in the world we all share.

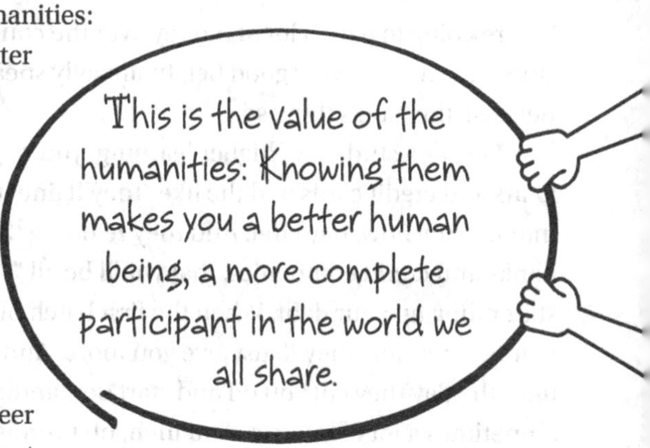
This is the value of the humanities: Knowing them makes you a better human being, a more complete participant in the world we all share.

And as a bonus, knowing the humanities can work for you in almost any career path that you choose. The study of history might include the study of the history of your specific career path. Knowledge of music or the arts can give you something to talk about at that business lunch. Being multilingual, in today's smaller world, is just necessary. And honestly, knowing how to write and communicate effectively is a prerequisite for advancement in nearly any field.

And on a personal note? Knowing literature and song and drama make romance a little easier. Understanding history and classics—the world then—makes it a little easier to understand our world now. And really, how awesome will you be to your kids (or nieces, or nephews, or whatever) if you can recite Lewis Carroll's *Jabberwocky* from memory?

So here's the thing: You don't *have* to embrace the humanities, but you should. If nothing else, it will give you the opportunity to know all the cool little stuff (like that the title of this piece was taken from the famous utterance of the reporter covering the Hindenburg and its ensuing disastrous crash) that makes your education—and life in general—a little sweeter.

6. Debt and U

Advice from a
Professor...

Congratulations—you have enormous potential.

You're going to earn a lot of money over the course of your lifetime. As a college student, you are a very good bet, financially speaking. How do we know this? Because the banks think so.

See, as a student of higher learning, you're going to get a lot of offers for loans and credit cards and the like. They'll line up to throw money at you: easy money. Buy now, pay later. And they're doing that because they know, those banks and credit companies, that you'll be all "Whoo-hoo! Free money!" and start piling up your debt. When the first batch of money has gone to beer and that new iPhone, they'll just give you more. And more. And more. More, that is, until the day they cut you off and start demanding it back, with interest. Sometimes a lot of interest. And then, oh promising youth? Then they own you.

Someone in your life might tell you that student loans are a good investment. That's sort of true. It was definitely true 30 years ago, when school was relatively cheap and the odds were good that you'd walk into a sweet job after four years of dorm life and classes. But financial times have certainly changed since the 80s, and educational finances are no different.

Student loans can be a good thing, for sure—they allow many students to go to college who wouldn't otherwise be financially able to do so. But don't go overboard with borrowing—taking out a loan for tuition is one thing. Taking out a loan to help you buy a car? Maybe not. Taking out a loan in order to fund a road trip for your friends to see the Harry Potter Experience in Orlando? No.

Subsidized loans are the best—that means the government is paying the interest while you're in school, so inflation works in your favor.

Unsubsidized loans from the government often have low interest rates, but don't be fooled—someone is still making money off these things, and it sure isn't you.

Hey! Did you just zone out a little bit when you read the words *subsidized, interest,* and *inflation*? Yeah, I know it can be boring stuff, especially if you're one of those people who just don't care for math. But, well . . . tough. You're not in high school anymore. You're an adult. (You can tell because you are over 18, are allowed to enter into contracts, and will be held to them.) You're no longer in high school, and dumb is no longer cool. Take the time to learn about your financial life now; you'll need it even more when you graduate and want to buy a house. Or at the very least, no one will be able to take advantage of your ignorance.

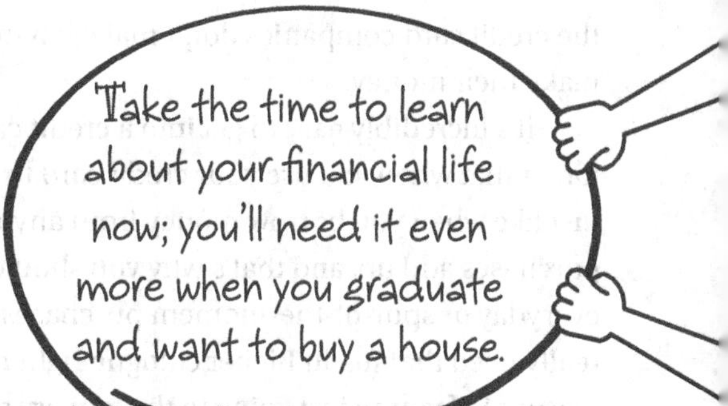
Take the time to learn about your financial life now; you'll need it even more when you graduate and want to buy a house.

Let's work the numbers . . .

If in your freshman year you take out a $10,000 loan at 5% annual interest, that means that in addition to that original $10,000, you'll be paying .05 (that's your interest rate in decimal form) times 10,000 (your original loan, otherwise known as your principal), divided by 365 (the number of days in a year). That equals $1.37 and is what you're paying every day for that loan; that adds up quick: that's $41.67 a month, $500 a year. And that's just the interest—even if you pay $500 a year toward that bill, you haven't even touched the original loan amount.

And it doesn't stop there. Assuming that you're not making payments each year (and most don't, because the loans don't require it until you graduate), the amount of the loan goes up. After one year, it's $10,500, which will cost you $525 in interest for the second year. After the second year, you owe $11,025, which will cost you $551.25 for the third year. After that third year, that $10K will have grown to $11,576.25 . . . and you're still at least a year away from graduating. The numbers only keep going up.

While it's important to know the numbers, you still shouldn't let that scare you. Many students come away from college with at least a bit of debt from student loans. Not the end of the world. What you have to be careful of, though, is credit card debt.

Not that credit cards themselves are bad—they're actually a necessary evil, because if you want to buy a house, or a car, or whatever else your own personal American Dream is made of, having a credit card is the only real way to establish and maintain your credit. The problem comes in their misuse—and the credit card companies don't make it hard to misuse them. That's how they make their money.

It's incredibly easy to get into a credit card hole—because it can be easy to forget that when you use your credit card to buy that case of PBR, that's debt. Just like when you borrow money from anyone for anything. But those little purchases add up, and that's why you shouldn't use your credit card for any everyday or spur-of-the-moment purchases. You might think you really really really need that Justin Bieber cologne right now, but you don't (for so many reasons). If you're just going to the grocery store for a few things, leave the credit card at home. Get into the habit of paying cash for things—with cash, you can't spend what you don't have. If you run across something you really need—whether something is worth going into debt for should be your test of "necessity"—then you can always come back with your credit card later.

The best way to use a credit card (and yes, you should have one, to establish credit) is to find one that has a reasonable APR (annual percentage rate). Definitely under 20%. Under 15% if you can find it. Don't worry about the credit limit—you shouldn't get anywhere near that cap if you're using it responsibly; besides, the credit card companies love raising your limit if you ask (so long as you've been good about establishing decent credit in the past). The best way to raise your credit score is to use your card a few times a month, and pay it off in full at the end of the month. On time, all the time. Late payments will cost you money in the form of penalties, and they lower your credit rating overall, which makes it tougher to get credit later.

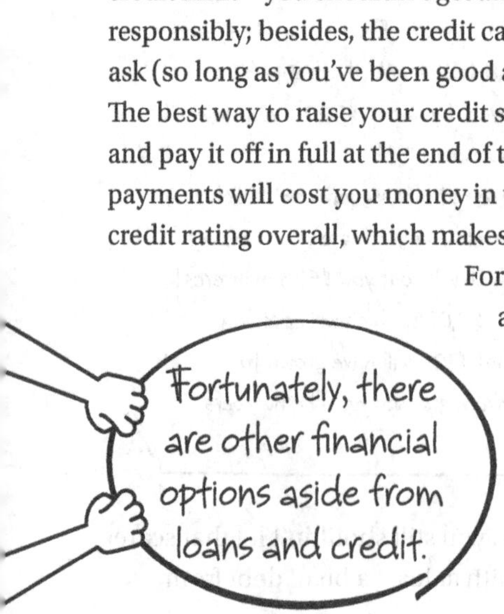
Fortunately, there are other financial options aside from loans and credit.

Fortunately, there are other financial options aside from loans and credit. (No, I'm not talking about Mom and Dad—I presume you're probably overdrawn there already.) Your first stop is your advisor, preferably for your major. Ask them straight up how you can get more money for school—they usually have the inside track on a lot of options you'd never be able to find out about: scholarships, grants, work-study. (These three options translate as free money, free money, and easy money respectively . . . none of which has to be paid back, ever.) If they can't help you, ask them to direct you to someone who can. There's always someone who knows.

And after all this, you'll still probably make some mistakes along the way. When that happens—and it happens to everyone sooner or later—the one rule you should follow is this: Don't ignore it. Hoping that it will go away never, ever works. That's actually the worst thing you can do. Stay in touch with your creditors, and don't let them bully you. Bankers might have tiny, black hearts, but they can often be talked into offering you some slightly less impossible options. They'd rather work with you than have to write you off as bad debt.

America is definitely the land of opportunity, which includes the opportunity for debt. But capitalism is all about moving money around. And debt itself isn't so bad, if you make it work for you. College is expensive—both the university tuition and the social life that goes along with it—and chances are you might need a little financial help. You're borrowing against your future, but your future is bright . . . as long as you're not stupid about it, you can afford it all.

7. Between Boredom and Terror

Six Steps to Financial Aid Solvency

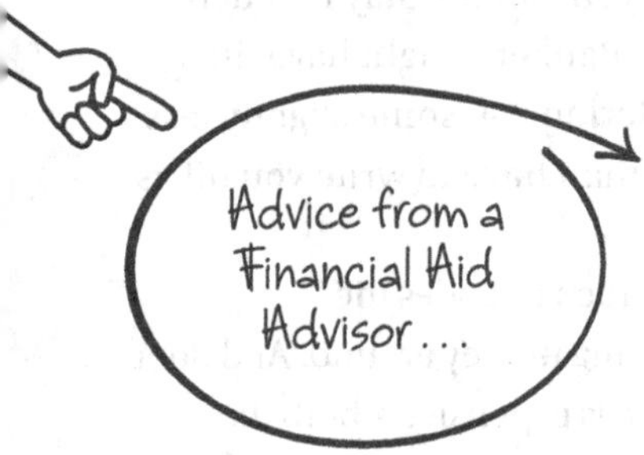
Advice from a
Financial Aid
Advisor...

Financial aid would be boring . . . if it weren't so terrifying.

Labyrinthine federal laws regulate complex need-determining equations. Important dates come and go. Thousands of dollars gush in and out of bank accounts. At best, financial aid is a bridge that connects you to the education you desire. At worst, it is a confusing, debt-inducing albatross that hangs around your neck and drags down your lifelong financial security.

Given the stakes involved, it makes sense to arm yourself with a little knowledge before making what is likely the first major investment in your life. That knowledge probably won't make financial aid any less yawn inducing, but it might scare you a little less.

Find a Financial Fit

Maybe you chose your dream school based on its reputation for academic rigor. Or its iconic architecture. Or its championship beer-pong team. But one consideration that is often lost in the glare of glossy admission brochures is whether you can actually afford the school you want to attend.

In the world of college admissions, counselors advise students to apply to schools that fall into three categories that reflect the likelihood of being admitted: reach schools, likely schools, and safety schools. But there is one more category that financial aid advisors add to that list: financial safety schools.

But finding a good financial fit isn't as easy as looking up a school's total cost of attendance and making sure that number is only mildly heart-attack inducing. What you really need to know is your net cost of attendance: how much you will have to pay out of pocket after the financial aid you've been offered has been applied to the bill.

To help estimate your net cost, most colleges provide a net price calculator. That means you should be able to go to just about any college's net price calculator website, enter your financial information, and receive an estimate of the federal funds for which you may be eligible. That total is then subtracted from the cost of attendance of your selected university. The remaining amount is what you would be expected to pay for with savings, scholarships, or private loans.

As helpful as that sounds, the results of a net price calculator can be misleading. Schools are only required to use the Department of Education's basic net price calculator template. That means your estimated net cost would not include awards like institutional merit-based scholarships, because the generic version does not account for the funds awarded by individual universities.

And even if the calculator is customized to account for things like merit-based awards, changes in awarding policies and the amount of funding available can skew the results.

The lesson here? You should deeply consider the cost of a university before committing to attend there. But you shouldn't let the sticker price of a school scare you away from applying for a school. Some high-cost private institutions have endowments that can bring the net cost of attendance down to an affordable level. Some public schools have very little funding to contribute. And you won't truly know which one you are dealing with until you receive an official award letter from your university.

The Whooshing Sound of Deadlines

The late author Douglas Adams said of deadlines that he loved "the whooshing sound they make as they fly by." When it comes to financial aid, that whooshing sound is accompanied by the sound of money being sucked out of your pocket.

Mundane as it sounds, meeting your school's financial aid deadlines can make thousands of dollars of difference in your award package.

Mundane as it sounds, meeting your school's financial aid deadlines can make thousands of dollars of difference in your award package. The reason is simple: Resources are limited, so priority is given to students who meet the deadlines.

And honestly? It's good practice for when you have to meet the real deadlines of financial aid—the monthly payback that you'll make later. (Never let this payback fall far from your mind when you're taking out loans—it may seem like free money now, but once you've graduated and the bills start coming due, it'll feel far from it. Make sure that the things you pay for with borrowed money are things you won't regret paying for later.)

Some Strings Attached

Leaving for college can feel like you've finally cut the apron strings. But the way the federal government sees it, you're still connected by purse strings.

For better or worse, the financial aid system is based on the idea that your parents have a greater responsibility than your college or the government to pay for your education. For this reason, the vast majority of undergraduate students are considered "dependents" for financial aid purposes. That means in order to complete the almost universally used financial aid application called the FAFSA (Free Application for Federal Student Aid), you are most likely going to need your parental tax information.

There is a short list of items that can qualify you as a financial aid "independent" and free you from having to bug your parents into supplying the required info. The most common ones are being 24 years old or older, being a veteran, being a graduate student, being married, or having a child.

Barring those qualifications, you'll be considered a dependent student and will be forced to make small talk with your mom.

Know Where to Puke

There are costs beyond tuition and fees associated with being a student. Items like meals, housing, and transportation may not show up on your bill, but you'll still have to pay for them while you are a student. So stick the basics: books, food, shelter, and, if possible, public transportation.

There are costs beyond tuition and fees associated with being a student.

I know a spring break vacation feels like a necessity when everyone you know is in Cancun taking off their tops and horking up Jose Cuervo. But consider that if you borrow

$2000 for your excursion, it will cost you $50 a month for 10 years after you graduate, and you will end up paying an extra $250 for the privilege of borrowing it. Better to save your money and puke in the comfort of your own home.

Borrow Cheaper Money First

When it comes to student loans, there are two main flavors: federal and private. Like it sounds, federal loans are provided by the federal government. And private loans come from banks. There are advantages and drawbacks to both types of loans, but in most scenarios it is preferable to borrow federal loans before taking out private loans.

That's due to the fact that federal loans have fixed interest rates, payments can be deferred until after graduation, and repayment can be based on your income. On the other hand, private loans often have variable interest rates, payments may start while you are still in school, and lenders are not obligated to give you a break on repayment just because your paycheck barely covers rent and ramen.

Do keep in mind that federal loans have annual limits that may not be enough to cover all of your expenses. (For a dependent freshman student, the current limit as of this writing is $5500.) So you still might end up needing a private loan. Just make sure you take the deal the government gives you first.

Forget the Car Dealership Mentality

Most schools will not negotiate on the financial aid award package because they don't have to. Universities have wait-lists full of potential enrollees who won't try to argue for additional funding, so students have very little leverage. Sure, you can ask for your school for more money. But don't be surprised when they say no.

However, if your family's financial situation has changed for the worse since submitting the financial aid applications, you should consider filing a financial aid appeal. A job loss, reduction of wages, extensive medical costs, and divorce are all situations that may qualify for a reassessment of your financial aid award. Every school has its own process for handling extenuating circumstances, so it is best to contact the financial aid office and find out what they need from you in order to proceed with an appeal.

Keep in mind that none of these rules mean that you should make your decisions in college solely based on finances, from where you go to how you live once you're there.

But finances are a part of the deal, just like they will be for the rest of your life, and it's important to take this first financial foray into the real world . . . well, seriously. Money matters might be boring, and they might be scary, but they're also the foundation for the adult life that you're working toward in the first place.

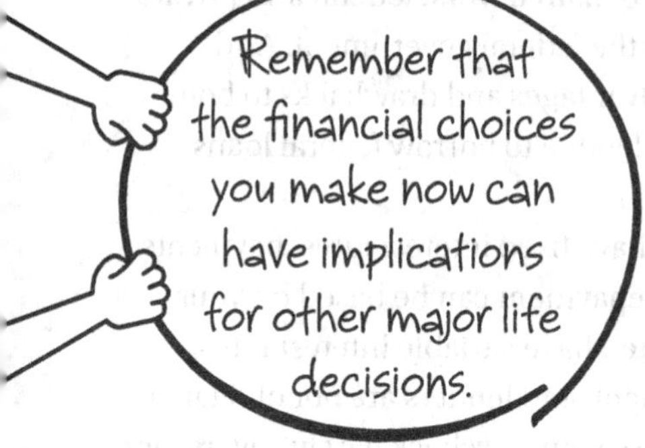
Remember that the financial choices you make now can have implications for other major life decisions.

One last thing: Remember that the financial choices you make now can have implications for other major life decisions. Things like purchasing a car, buying a house, and planning your retirement. Or taking that vacation to Cancun and puking on your own dime.

Sandra Mizumoto Posey

8. Why Choosing a Major for Stupid Reasons Might Be a Very Smart Thing to Do

Advice from a Professor and Administrator . . .

I have a Ph.D. in folklore. Let's start right there. You really can't choose more foolishly than that. And I have never had trouble finding a job.

My friend Camilla, who has an undergrad degree in anthropology and a Ph.D. in comparative literature, now works as an environmental reporter for a regional alternative weekly newspaper. Emily, who majored in Asian studies, is now a career counselor. We were all, at one point, young and foolish and passionate. We chose majors in college, and even in graduate school, that didn't have a clear path afterward—either toward a career, or toward any real way to make money (read: pay off student loans). While we may not be as young anymore, age has taught us that we weren't so foolish after all. We all have jobs we love. We all made careers out of majors that were in no real way vocational.

This should tell you several things:

1. **If you pursue what you love in college, that passion translates into academic success.** Academic success demonstrates to people—often in fields you never imagined you'd enter—that you're capable of meeting, if not exceeding, expectations. It indicates that you care about what you do, you invest in it, and you aren't willing to settle for less than the best. That's a quality employers want. Awesome. So your degree isn't useless after all.
2. **Job markets change.** A major that lines you up for a specific career path may leave you hanging when that industry ceases to exist or changes drastically. There is, on the other hand, very little industry associated with a lot of majors (like the ones listed in the first paragraph). Most people would expect that the outcome of such majors is to teach . . . and sure, that

happens. But if you ask around, a lot of the really interesting jobs, the ones that you find difficult to identify a clear major for, have at their helm people with impractical degrees. The people in those jobs are ones that often took circuitous (and interesting!) paths to get there.

3. **Passions change over the course of a lifetime.** You may not always find the same things interesting that you do now. Choose a major that ignites your passions now but also one that will teach you critical thinking skills (the ability to comprehend information, analyze it, evaluate it, and apply it). Most majors will do this; the difference is, if you are passionate about the subject matter, you will learn the skills that are being taught along with the material. These transferable skills are ones that you can apply to the many fields and many passions you may encounter along the way.

You may not always find the same things interesting that you do now.

4. **People who think outside of the box find boxes to fill.** Know what you are capable of. After a good college education, that's a lot. Just because you end up with a supposedly impractical degree, or even if you end up with one that is practical (hopefully because your ever-passionate heart loved that practical subject), *don't limit your career possibilities to jobs that are directly related to your major*. Apply widely but with targeted letters that demonstrate how what you learned is relevant to the job you are applying for.

5. **Being foolish may be the wisest thing you ever do.** Foolish people, ones who pursue the study of a subject for no other reason than that they love it, are happy people. Emily, Camilla, and I (and thousands like us) continue to be foolish. We become passionate about things no one else might consider interesting. The economy finds places for passionate people.

6. **Even if you don't know what your passion is yet, college is the perfect place to find one.** Professors are just the sort of people who followed their passions. Pay attention to them and see if one of their passions doesn't rub off on you a little bit. And in a more GPA-mercenary way, one terrific side benefit to letting a professor's passion rub off on you is that you'll probably get a good grade in the course.

So in a difficult job market, the best advice I can give you is to be foolish. What you choose to study isn't necessarily what defines you—rather, it's how you study, how committed to it you are, how hard you work at it. So yes, you can be passionate, be crazy, and take chances . . . and take the world by unpredictable storm.

Sandra Mizumoto Posey

9. Why Professors Want to Help You

Your Professor May Have Been a Loser Too (Part 1)

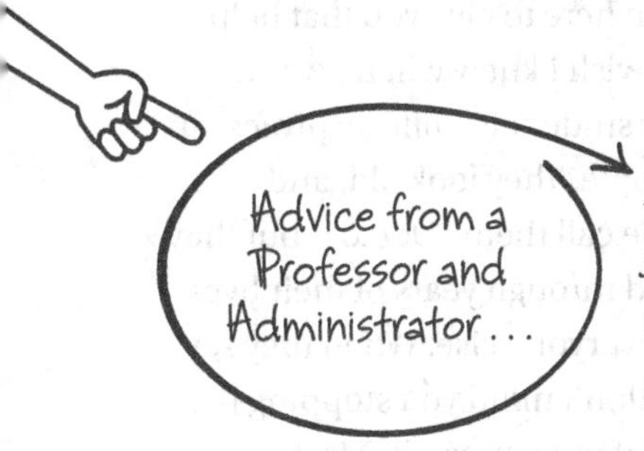

I'm a professor. I have a Ph.D. and a big fancy title, but that doesn't mean I don't remember being a student, remember being where you are. What it does seem to mean, though, is that you don't know who I am. Not at all.

For example, you probably wouldn't expect that I was such a loser in high school. I was a bright, happy student in elementary school, but somewhere around sixth grade, hormones hit and all of a sudden I didn't know how to make friends. Zits, braces (yes, even headgear), social awkwardness—you name the awful, maladjusted teenage stereotype and I was plagued with it. It affected my grades too. I failed algebra; I got kicked out of French for reading other books during class. By sixteen I almost OD'd on Midol. (Listen, I've never claimed to be a genius.) Not long afterward I dropped out of high school altogether. I didn't have a plan, and certainly not one for college. My parents hadn't gone to college, so they didn't have any advice for me. They let me live at home, but otherwise I had to figure it out myself. For a couple of years I waitressed (badly—I spilled hot food on people), worked retail, and tried on a religion or two, until I finally started dipping my toes into community college. I had **no** idea who I was or what I was going to do with my life.

So yeah, if you feel like a fraud, like everyone will figure out that you're clueless and scared about your first year in college, don't worry. Some of us were scared and clueless too. You may even be better off than I was—you may have had someone giving you good advice about how important college was or how to get into the good ones—but it's not likely you're starting off college any worse. And even if you are starting out on a worse foot than I did, it doesn't mean you won't succeed. Your professors are there to help you get there. You just have to take that first step and show them you have the initiative and drive that means their advice won't go in one ear and out the other.

You should know that when I say come to my office hours and talk to me, I mean it. It doesn't mean I want to hear your sob stories as some excuse for why you didn't get your homework in on time, but you can bet that if you need help with figuring out what's going on in class, I'm here to give you that help.

This is what I wish I knew when I was a first-year student in college: professors are people.

This is what I wish I knew when I was a first-year student in college: professors are people. They look old, and people call them "Doctor," but they flailed through years of their lives like everyone else. When they say they don't mind you stopping by, most of them mean it. Most of us wish more students would take us up on it. Office hours are lonely.

Honestly? Most of us are kind of tired of students treating us like we're aliens from the planet of fancy degrees. Sure, we might like you calling us "Doctor," but that's only because we may still be clinging to the title that helped us forget we were such losers in high school. And about school: Regardless of whether we were A students in school or failing ones, we eventually spent enough time there to have finally mastered it. So seek out our help. We have secrets and we're willing to share.

10. Why Professors Want to Help You

Your Professor May Have Been a Loser Too (Part 2)

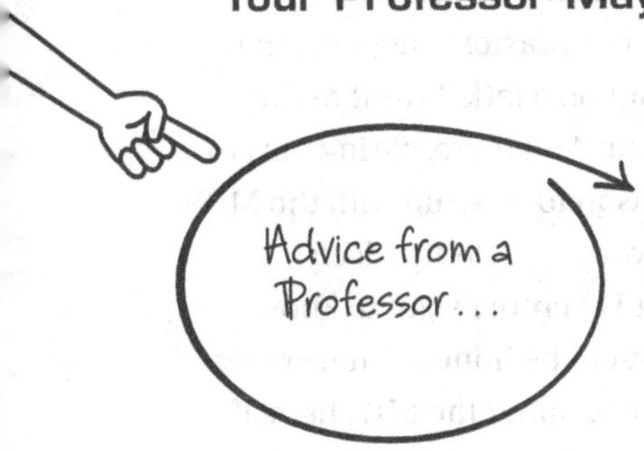
Advice from a Professor . . .

I'm also a professor. And despite what some students seem to think, I wasn't born this way.

I was once a student too, wandering around hallways, trying to find my classes on time, forcing myself to get up (most mornings) and drag myself to class after a long night of whatever. Cramming for tests. Studying things I didn't always appreciate, and some things I found surprisingly amazing. And, in the end, wondering if I was doing any of it right.

Here's the big lesson of higher education: the only way to do it wrong is to stop working at it. To drop out, to stop attending classes, to stop having some faith that there's a point to it all or an end to that academic road that's worth the travelling. There is an end to that road, and it's a better place than you were without that degree. You just have to keep walking.

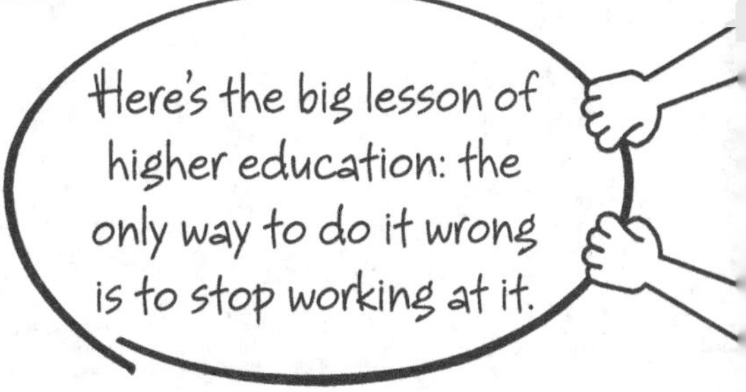
Here's the big lesson of higher education: the only way to do it wrong is to stop working at it.

But for me, like for many of you, the road was long and winding. I didn't start out my college career with the thought that I'd study writing and eventually teach it at the college level. It was a lot less stellar a start than that, believe me.

To be frank, I became a college professor for the usual reason: a girl. No, really. I'd already figured out that I might want to teach, and I'd stumbled through a bachelor's degree. (After changing majors four times, I finally graduated through some miracle of scheduling in four years, with a degree in creative writing.) The plan was to teach English in high school; seemed like a noble profession, and so I enrolled in a postbaccalaureate program for secondary ed. At the same time, I'd applied for the Masters of Fine Arts program in creative writing, and got invited to go do that too.

But I wasn't planning to accept. I was already a semester into the postbac program and was liking it just fine. It wasn't a Master's degree, but it was a career path, and I was already on my way. But on a lark, I went to the orientation meeting for the MFA, just to check it out. And there, sitting next to me, was a girl. And honestly, she was more the reason for staying with the MFA than I'd like to admit. Bad idea? Certainly. Did it work out? Pretty nicely.

The romantic in me would like to tell you that I eventually got to know that girl, married her, and started a life together. But to be honest, I never saw her again. (Who knows—maybe she was on the fence about the MFA herself, and decided against it because of the weird dude who was sitting next to her at orientation.) But that's OK; she'd done me a great favor.

And my story isn't all that unusual. The details change, but the academic road is always surprising in some pretty big ways. Always. And that gives most professors a lot of sympathy for you, on that intellectual road of your own. We've been there, and believe me when I say that it doesn't feel all that long ago, even if it's been decades.

So, remember: Professors have more to teach than just their subjects. There is no one correct road to where you're going, and we know that too. If you let us help direct you a bit . . . oh, the places you'll go.

section two

In Class, with Class

"It's good to have students sit near the front. However ..."

Andrewgenn/Fotolia

Teague von Bohlen

11. Choose Your Seat Wisely

The Strategy of Sitting Well in the Classroom

So it's your first day of college classes—you've found a place to park your car, walked across campus, and found the right building and the right room. Now comes your first big decision, one that's going to establish you as a student whether you realize it or not: choosing where to sit.

Stay with me here.

It might seem overly simple, but remember: This isn't high school anymore, and assigned seats are by and large a thing of the past. (Honestly, if you ever get a prof who requires that you sit in some sort of planned organization, take advantage of the inside knowledge you now have as to their OCD condition.) When you walk into a college classroom, it's up to you to find your seat—and where in the room you choose to position yourself is going to say a lot about you as a student.

Your Convenience

First and foremost, you're going to want a seat that offers what you need in the way of practical matters. That might mean proximity to an exit: You may need to leave early, you might have a long walk across campus to get to your next class on time, or your bladder may not easily suffer a three-hour lecture without some attention. Or it might mean sitting up closer to the board, if you're completely unwilling to admit that you need glasses.

Here's the thing: Getting up and leaving in the middle of class is disruptive. Sometimes it's necessary (when you gotta go, you gotta go), but it's important to remember that it does interrupt. So do everything you can to minimize your exit—and if you ever know that you have to leave early (for an advising appointment or a doctor's visit that you couldn't schedule another time), let your professor know before class begins, so you don't risk a sad face in the grade book next to the note "cut out early." These sorts of things can have a direct effect on your final grade, if participation is considered. And even if it's not, the difference between a B+ and an A− is sometimes a judgment call. Always maximize your professorial goodwill!

Your Fears

Some students, hard working as they may be, are scared to death of class participation. Now this is a larger issue than simple seat selection can solve, but there are some tips that can help make sure that you don't get called on, if that's what you're going for. You might think that you're better off staying in the back, but that's far from the truth. In fact, those are the students who are going to get called on more often than not. The front row might be a good bet, but sometimes during a lecture a professor is just looking for some evidence that someone's listening, and so they'll most likely call on one of their go-to folks—and early in the term, they're going to assume that's the front row. Your best bet is to go peripheral: near the front, so you look engaged, but over to the side, where professors are less likely to notice you.

Some students, hard working as they may be, are scared to death of class participation.

Keep in mind that this strategy in no way prevents you from being graded down at the end of the term for not participating in class, if that's part of the final grade. If you have a class in which the prof specifies that class discussion and participation are part of your grade for the course, take that seriously, do yourself a favor, and forget this entire section. Thank you.

Your Prof

Here's the biggie: your professor probably assumes certain things based on where in the classroom you sit. If you're in the back, he or she will probably assume that you're disinterested, or wanting to get away with paying less attention, or hiding your iPod. If you're in the front, they'll assume that you're there to learn, that you enjoy participation, and that you're generally engaged. These are the spots that profs notice.

The middle area, however, is sort of the great-equalizer. It says very little about who you might be as a student, which gives you something of an edge. You can, at the very least, define who you are and what you can do based on your work . . . which is good or bad, depending on said work.

Keep in mind what your professor sees from his or her position at the front of the class. You want to be noticed, because professors are psychologically more generously inclined toward a student whom they recall not only by name, but by face . . . assuming that you work to keep your face awake, alert, and engaged.

Your Peers

Know that it's not only your professor who will judge you for your seat choice—so will your fellow students. Pay attention to where your classmates sit in class—if you're new to the course, and don't know the professor well, other students might know something you don't. For example, a professor who gets so excited about the subject that he or she sometimes spits a little will often have classes where students in the know sit no closer than the third row. Paying attention to this can save you an unnecessary and unwelcome shower.

Know that it's not only your professor who will judge you for your seat choice—so will your fellow students.

You also want to make sure that you take advantage of the culture of the classroom—if you're literally the only one in the back row, you're not going to meet anyone, not going to know how to reach them outside of class, and won't be able to contact them if you have a question or need notes. No man (or woman!) is an island—don't pretend to be one in class.

Given these four elements, it should be clear to you that choosing your seat should be given a little more thought than chair color or the relative gum-free level of your desk's underside.

Heather Joseph-Witham

12. Can I Sit Next to That Chick in the Burka?

Diversity in College Life

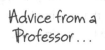

Advice from a Professor . . .

They were about as different from each other as you could imagine: two of my favorite students.

One was tatted-up and tough; he'd seen his share of trouble, you could tell, but he was trying to quit smoking. And even though he scared some of my colleagues, he was fun, sharp, and creative. My other student was a big guy, decidedly not cool in the way my first student was naturally. This second kid was tall and gawky—your typical geek. Video games, costumes, the works. Turns out, this unlikely pair of students were buddies, and good ones.

My first thought was, "thank goodness we're not in high school anymore." You know exactly what I mean. In high school no one can dare to befriend someone who is too much unlike them. It's scary and may make people (ugh) *look* at you. But college isn't supposed to be like that. This is the time to embrace the diverse. I'm not saying you have to go and convert religions, attend gothic vampire dances with those kids with the eyeliner, or eat organic brussels sprouts with the vegans. But give those who are different from you a chance. A real chance. Your contacts with those who are a little outside your comfort zone will likely turn out to be some of your most interesting in your college years. Will they be a bit scary? Sometimes. But you'll learn, and grow, from them.

Diversity covers a lot of ground, but at its root, it has to do with recognizing and appreciating differences in others. Age, status, ethnicity, race, sexual orientation, gender, political orientation, religion, learning styles, physical differences, hobbies . . . you name it. The list goes on.

There are books out there that explain the many cultural differences between people. For example, are you giving me the shaka "hang loose" hand signal, or are you flashing gang signs at me? Do Converse tennis shoes somehow signify sexual orientation? Why does the Jewish guy in your chemistry class have what appear to be strings hanging out of his shirt every day? For some things, the Internet can help! Look it up (but check your sources).

As for the day-to-day navigation of the complexities of diversity on a college campus? Here are a few tips:

1. **Never ask anyone what they are.** This is a sure way to offend. If you wonder if the girl you are talking to is Native American or Filipino, you are just going to have to wait to find out. Many a student has told me that this has happened to them and it did nothing but annoy them. Not a good first impression.
2. **Do not assume that anyone at your school is from the same political party as you.** Ever. You can bring politics up, but never fight, never scream about it. What for? It certainly won't change anyone else's mind and you may have lost a potentially good friend or acquaintance.
3. **It's OK to ask someone about their cultural customs—just do it in a sensitive way.** Can you tell me about K-Pop? What is Kim Chee made of? Why aren't you coming to school on Yom Kippur? Questions are better than judgmental statements any day of the week.
4. **Act like you're fine, even if you're initially uncomfortable with someone's sexual or gender orientation.** Fake it 'till you make it. Is it all right in the 21st century to discriminate? Well, you already know the answer to that. Still, you may be from a small town left of nowhere where all of the gay kids pretended that they weren't. But—yes they were! Now, in college, they feel like they can finally be themselves. It may take them a while to feel OK about being public, so don't make it hard on them. If you don't want someone asking you about your sexual preferences, don't ask someone else either (more on this in the chapter "Tasting the Rainbow, One Friend at a Time"). Be sensitive to the fact that your classmates may be experimenting, coming out for the first time, and may be having difficulties of their own. (And, if you're gay? Don't get too mad at the folks who claim they never met a homosexual. They really, really didn't know!)
5. **Don't assume you know something about someone else's religion.** Believe it or not, decades ago, upon finding out I was Jewish, a student asked where my horns and tail were. Really sad, but I did handle it with cool. This semester,

I have one Hare Krishna, several pagans, one Satanist, a variety of Christians, and two Muslims in one of my classes. All good folks, and all with amazing things to say about how they grew up and what they believe. Don't miss out on a potential friendship due to differing belief systems. The funny thing is that if you ask many people, they have a hard time telling you about what exactly it is that they believe—even if they belong to a specific religious group. Keep that in mind, keep an open mind, and be chill.

6. **Post nothing—I mean *nothing*—that could be construed negatively about other students and their diverse selves and diverse behaviors on social media.** One student came to me upset because another posted about her "Catholic attitudes" on Facebook based on an in-class discussion regarding the role of skepticism in belief cultures. Another professor took a class break and saw one of her students who just presented a paper in class run crying down the hall. It turns out another student tweeted about the "stupid-looking Barbie" who gave her paper. None of these students were friends or on each other's networks. Guess what—everyone has acquaintances in common and everyone will forward these comments. The commenter is the one who ends up looking awful—and probably feeling awful too.

7. **Check your lingo.** If you're in college, you should know by now that ethnic slurs are a big no-no. What you may not know is that there are *emic* or "insider" languages: terms that are OK for people within a specific group or culture, but might be a serious insult coming from outside that group or culture. For example, a group of gay men might call each other *queer* or say, "that is so *so* gay." But if you are hetero, that will sound different coming from you. Likewise, African Americans sometimes use racial epithets—again, to reverse their hurtful meanings and take the sting away—that no one else should ever use. I heard Koreans tease another Korean student and call her a FOB (fresh off the boat), a term that an outsider should

They go to discover themselves, to be a part of a community, to learn about people, to be a part of things they have never before experienced.

definitely not try out. I wasn't even familiar with that term, but at the time, the students swore they saw it as a descriptive term of endearment. If you're not an "insider," even if these are your besties, you can't use these terms. You might think it's totally not fair that they can use them and you can't—yes, students have said this to me. Too bad! Find other words. That's part of what your English class is for.

So, can you sit next to that chick in the burka? First of all, don't call her a chick—young lady will do! Secondly, she's in college. People don't go to college just to learn academics! They go to discover themselves, to be a part of a community, to learn about people, to be a part of things they have never before experienced. If she is there, you can sit there too and, yes, you can talk to her. She might be just as intimidated by your fraternity-lettered shirt as you are by her burka. I hope you both enjoy the conversation.

Sandra Mizumoto Posey

13. Get on the SyllaBus

Take a look at a college syllabus. Any college syllabus. The number one thing to learn from that document is that to every college professor, their subject is the most interesting in the world.

We professors wasted years of our lives getting a degree or two that says so, so we have to believe it or we'll kill ourselves with quill pens. Pretend you think so too (that the subject is interesting, not that we'll kill ourselves with outdated writing instruments) and you're already well on your way to a B.

All right, now back to that syllabus. Remember that any information on your syllabus is important. It's all there for a reason. Sure, it often seems like a long, cumbersome, obligatory document, but believe it or not we as faculty put some thought into this stuff. We may have even spent long hours crafting this document. Remember, we're convinced this is interesting.

OK, first, take note of the top of the page: you've got contact info. **Use it.** Go to office hours. If the professor knows you, you're now on your way to an A. Ask something about class, not just what'll be on the test. That bumps you back to a B. It's tempting to use email for quick questions, but that won't get you noticed. Showing up at office hours will. And while we're up there at the top of the page, notice the time the class begins. That means you're supposed to show up before then. Not right then; before then. Because being there is, you know, sort of requisite.

Ooh, next there's a course description. Sometimes it's a short description straight from the catalog. Fair warning: We may or may not follow that. (Call it academic freedom.) But pay special attention if the description is modified or developed. That's what your particular professor really thinks the class is about. This will give you some hints into the themes and overarching ideas the professor thinks are important. Whenever you're confused about what they are rambling on and on about in lecture or discussion, go back and remind yourself with this concise synopsis of what the class is supposed to be about. You may then be able to make sense of the lecture.

Then we have required readings. That means they're required, not just to buy, but to read. And we have tricks for finding out whether you really read them. We have superpowers and things like pop quizzes if you're annoying us. If you do happen upon a professor who doesn't seem to care that you haven't done the reading, it's because they have also stopped caring whether or not you fail. They figure that succeeding and failing is up to you and if you want to succeed you'll read. It's certainly not that they don't notice. We *know* when you've done the reading and when you haven't. And about those professors that don't care, they're right: succeeding *is* up to you.

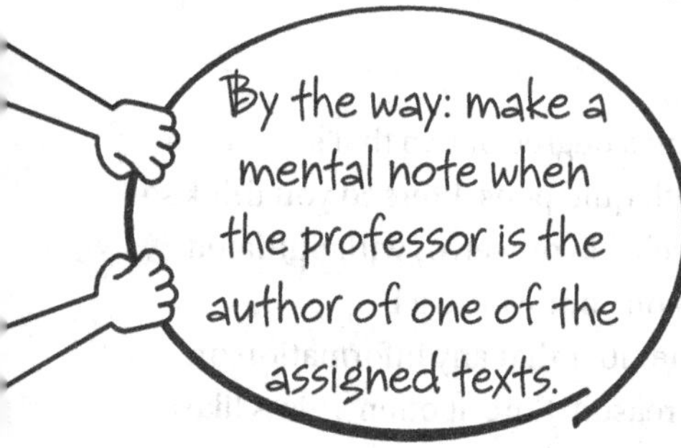
By the way: make a mental note when the professor is the author of one of the assigned texts.

By the way: make a mental note when the professor is the author of one of the assigned texts. Read that stuff once, twice, three times. If you don't understand it, ask questions. If you do understand it, ask questions. Either way, show some interest. This is that person's life work and it's like a stake to the heart when you don't care. When grading time comes around, no matter how well you did on tests, you don't want a stake in your professor's heart getting in the way of their hand entering that A you really deserve.

You might have a section that lays out, either with a broad brush or a meticulousness that verges on psychosis, what the class will cover each day. Note the very important caveat that will assuredly be on every course schedule (or if it isn't, assume that it is): These plans may change. They often will. Pay attention. If you're in class every day, you'll find out about these changes. If you're not, you may miss out on something critical and look like a dolt doing so. At the very least, you'll end up staying up until 4:42 a.m. for a paper that the professor gave the class another week to work on and make awesome. (And let's be frank: very little happens at 4:42 a.m. that could be considered awesome.)

Next there's a section you might just gloss over or ignore entirely if I didn't tell you this secret: For some professors it's the most important part of the syllabus. It's often called Student Learning Outcomes or Goals or Objectives something along those lines. This is everything, in a nutshell, your professor is hoping you get out of the class. Anytime you're confused, go back and ask yourself, "how does this random essay relate to these Outcomes?" The answer to that will usually tell you exactly the angle you should take in order to make that essay seem a little less random—both to you in the writing, and to your professor in its eventual reading (and grading).

After Outcomes there are probably Performance Measures or a Grading Rubric or something else breaking down specific percentages of how you'll be evaluated. This is how your professor will know whether you actually achieved those Student Learning Outcomes. Pay attention to how much of your grade will be determined by what. If 20 percent is participation, you'd darn well better show up and, well, participate. Otherwise, even if you ace the rest of the classwork, you could end up with a B. Worse yet, if you don't show up or if you mentally check out during class, it will likely affect other parts of your grade beyond that 20% because you'll miss key points *and* your professor will likely take a less kindly eye toward the rest of your work.

Often at this point there will be a section about plagiarism and cheating. Professors all hope this is common sense, but we've taught long enough and had our hearts broken often enough that we know it's not. But really, just don't do it. (More on this elsewhere in this book, where we'll go more in depth than "just don't do it." But really, that oughta suffice, shouldn't it?)

Finally on most syllabi there's a calendar or schedule that tells you what's going to happen on what day. This is the part of the syllabus most students actually pay some attention to, but if you haven't read the rest of the syllabus, you may lose out on why something is important or how it fits into the overall picture of the course and the subject being taught. The schedule is the list of ingredients. The rest of the syllabus is the recipe. A list of ingredients alone will never make a finished dish. You have to know how to put it all together.

So when your professor rambles on, seeming random, disjointed, or crazy, remember he or she is actually trying to make a point. If you pay attention to the professor and to the syllabus, you may learn what that point is. You may even earn an A. If you're very lucky, you might just learn why the professor fell in love with this subject in the first place.

So when your professor rambles on, seeming random, disjointed, or crazy, remember he or she is actually trying to make a point.

14. TXT L8R

Technology can be a wonderful thing. It's brought about a new information age, a time in which almost anything—for good and bad—is at our fingertips.

It's a great resource . . . and a great time waster. For every great step (the convenience of email), there's a negative (spam). And really, who among us wouldn't rather the term *apps* refer to yummy party snacks involving cocktail wieners and toothpicks?

Likewise, technology has its place in the classroom, both as a teaching and learning tool . . . and a distraction. One sure way to leave a negative impression on your professor, for example, is to spend the entire class session clutching your phone in a thumb-typing frenzy. Hiding the phone between your knees does not help. Holding it to your side as you fire off a few quick text messages is not as inconspicuous as you may think. Even if you have the forethought to put the phone on vibrate, the buzz of the reply from the person on the other end of the conversation doesn't go unnoticed by your professor and it is quite distracting for your classmates in close proximity. Refrain. Tell the person on the other end of that phone that you'll text him or her back right after class.

Practice safe learning. We all know that texting while driving is dangerous. Anyone who is texting and driving is distracted from the road, is less observant of their surroundings, and exhibits slower reaction times to obstacles. Texting while learning carries similar consequences. Texting during class prevents you from paying attention to what is being taught, makes you less aware of the contributions made by your classmates, and limits your ability to meaningfully participate in discussions and answer questions. Professors notice and remember this, especially if you are unprepared when called upon.

Many, many years ago in the dim times of the 1980s, the ability to send text-based messages from one mobile phone to the next became possible. The service was referred to as Short Message Service or SMS. The number of characters that could be sent in each message was limited by the technology that existed. Service providers also charged by the amount of data used by the consumer or the number of messages sent per billing cycle—meaning you could get charged for both sending and receiving text messages! People who used the texting service grew very creative with how they conveyed a complete thought in attempts to minimize the costs of their own usage and to respect that of their text recipients. Every character counted. So, to an even greater degree than telegrams before them (which tended to just drop "helper" words), a very terse form of communication was born: grammatically correct sentences were replaced with consonant-only words (such as *txt*), phonetically spelled expressions (such as *roxowt,* which represents "rocks out"), symbols in place of words (such as <3, which means "love"), and acronyms that represent an entire phrase (such as *lol,* which means "laughing out loud"). As the shortened language became more and more terse and cryptic, its readability became more exclusive, so much so that it was termed "Leet" or "l33+" speak, short for "elite."

What was once a form of communication used only in informal and social spaces suddenly crept into academic settings, much to the dismay of teachers and professors everywhere. All lowercase sentences, missing punctuation, deliberate misspellings, and casual language have become more prevalent in learning environments. We are not amused. So pls dnt uz txt spk wn sndng m@l 2 ur prof.

Digital communication has become commonplace between student and professor in many situations—but you always have to be careful. Always refrain from using text language, *even in a text message*! Use of texting nomenclature does not offer a professional tone and does not communicate how seriously you are taking the course, your level of respect for the academic environment, or your understanding that there should be a difference in how you interact in social and professional settings. There is a time and place for everything. Knowing the "when" and "where" for each type of correspondence is important.

Digital communication has become commonplace between student and professor in many situations—but you always have to be careful.

I once had a brilliant student who turned in excellent work. He asked clarifying questions over email and sent follow-up communications after class discussions. The problem was, his emails were all composed in text language. I often had to look up what a set of symbols meant in order to reply to him. Finally, I asked him to use his academic "voice" when emailing with me and other professors. He responded by stating that I was attempting to stifle his identity and that he did not find his use of text language unprofessional at all. I then advised him to rewrite his resume in "elite" speak and submit it to potential employers to see how many call backs he would receive. He got the message.

One last warning about technology in the classroom: Don't misuse your technology in class. The laptop (or tablet computer, smart phone, etc.) is now a welcomed tool in many college classrooms. Professors who invite students to bring such hardware—or hold class in computer labs—realize the value of allowing learners to type notes, have access to software and applications needed for the course, and augment class discussions with resources found on the Internet. This permission to bring technology to class does not mean that your professors encourage email reading, unrelated Internet browsing, instant messaging, or game play during instruction. I once had a student who seemed to be diligently typing notes as I presented the concept of social cognitive learning to the class. His intent tapping on his keyboard seemed studious and appropriate. It wasn't until I asked the class to get into groups and share their opinions of the assigned readings that I became aware that the student wasn't taking notes after all. His continued keyboarding—when he should have been talking or listening—made me curious about what had his attention. As I moved close and glanced over his shoulder, I learned that he was in a heated World of Warcraft battle, an online multiplayer game. I told the student that he should be working with his group. He told me that he just needed a few more minutes to "level." That incident immediately told me what "level" his grade would be for that class session. It was only surprising that he didn't know . . . but he found out, and his grade ended up being far from "elite."

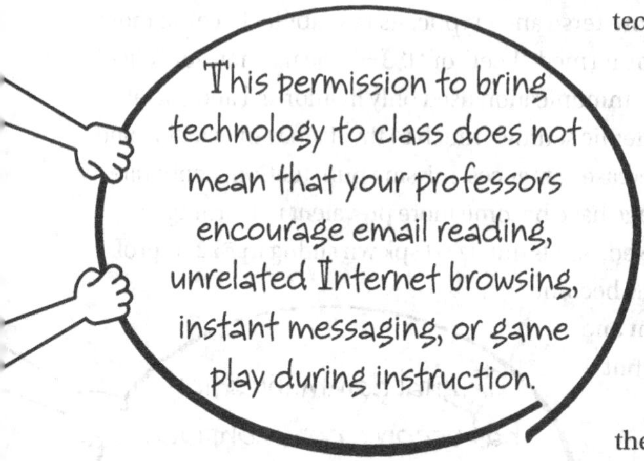
This permission to bring technology to class does not mean that your professors encourage email reading, unrelated Internet browsing, instant messaging, or game play during instruction.

Victoria Simmons

15. How Pretending to Be Interested Is Good for Everyone

I'm writing this essay to ask you please please to continue pretending to be interested in class. You see how serious I am: I've even spelled everything out 4U and used spell-check.

OK, this is it. I know you're not really interested in class. Why would you be? It's not like class is interesting. It might surprise you to hear it, but most of these things you do that you think are OK? Other people find them annoying, even if they do those same things themselves. The flip is also true, of course: You know that stuff other people do that drives you batty? You probably do that stuff too.

Oops.

Well, what's the biggie? It's not like you're grabbing your top hat and cane, and singing and dancing up and down the aisles. It's not even like you're just breaking out the phone and having a good old chat with your sister right there in front of everybody. How distracting can what you're doing possibly be? It's just one person, opening and closing things, getting things out and putting them away, turning things on and off. Not much, right?

Except, of course, it's distracting. All by yourself, you're a little symphony of SNAP-POP SHPRITZ SHUFFLE-SHUFFLE-SHUFFLE ZIIIIIP!!, with your own glowing blue aura from your phone.

Yes, you're just being you. You don't think about it, and you don't really even think about it when someone else is doing it—even though you make a face or roll your eyes or shake your head as though flicking off a mosquito. You don't think it bothers other people, and you don't think that what other people are doing bothers you either. I mean, not to the point that it interferes with listening or taking notes. You're used to it. And, anyway, who really listens? Or needs amazing notes, either? You're floating around in your own bubble, and everything is cool.

And doesn't it make you more interesting to be the person who's always late, always in crisis, always go go go, and forgetting things and dropping things, and things falling out of your arms and bag and pockets as you go, but so plugged in that you're always up to the minute on who's saying or doing what to whom? No. Actually, it doesn't make you more interesting, because there are a lot of people like that. And that may make it seem like it's the right way to be, but the funny thing is that while people find their own flakiness intriguing, they tend to find it annoying in other people. What they really like and admire in other people is the boring stuff: being dependable and on time, not flaky and annoying and distracting. That's true of your instructor, who is becoming a bitter old fogey at the age of 35 because of all the inconsiderate students in her life. It's true of your fellow students, who are perpetually scattered and exhausted, and don't know why. And it's true of you, too.

What they really like and admire in other people is the boring stuff: being dependable and on time, not flaky and annoying and distracting.

Not being a pain in the ass isn't sucking up or being a teacher's pet. It's just not being a pain in the ass. Give it a try. If you try to get out of the house at 7:15, and that still doesn't get you to class on time, then leave by 7:00. Pick up the next day's in-class snacks on the way out, and keep them in your car. Anything that slows you down, find a way around it. Make it a game, if that helps. Anything that makes noise or otherwise distracts, find a way around it. Open the chips and the soda before you go into the classroom. If you are entering the room late, get out what you'll need before going in, so you don't have to go through the whole production number while the instructor and the other students are trying to focus on the matters at hand. If you have to leave early, sit near the door.

What's weird is that doing the stuff you should do and not doing the stuff you shouldn't do—just to be polite, just so the instructor won't deduct pain-in-the-ass points from your participation grade, just so your fellow students will think you've got it pulled together—actually **helps** you get it all pulled together. Life feels simpler, you feel less scattered. It's easier to concentrate and focus. You understand more. The fakery involves learning to pretend to be attentive, to feign interest, to laugh convincingly at others' jokes, and to learn to keep the look of interest pasted on your face while studying or composing texts in your head. A bit of practice at this will prepare you for future career success in pretending to be interested. And you're right: You may find that pretending to be interested turns into actually being interested. Not always, not in everything. But enough that you start doing better. The world starts making a little more sense to you. This might require further fakery in concealing from the cool kids that you are genuinely interested, but the results are probably worth it. And you may find that being interested makes you more interesting to others.

Here's the thing: It's not going to ruin your life if you continue into your career with the late thing, the noisy thing, the multitasking thing, and in general the half-assed thing. After all, it's a half-assed, multi-tasking sort of world. And you live your life honestly, you are who you are, and isn't that what you've been taught to be? But here's the other thing: The half-assed you probably isn't the you you would prefer to be. With a little bit of effort and a little bit of faking it, you can create a good-student persona that will help carry you successfully through school, prepare you for a good-employee persona you will maintain with the greatest of ease throughout your career, make it easier for you to flake without serious repercussions when you genuinely need to flake, and—who knows?—perhaps even turn you into a more focused, *better* student and employee, and a happier, more successful human being.

I know you're worried about not being up-to-the-second with everything that's happening. But, ooh, imagine a world in which you're able to focus and concentrate.

Think hard before giving it a try. I don't want to turn your life upside down or anything. But I do want to warn you about the dangers of pretending to be interested. I mean, who knows? It's so easy for pretending to be interested to turn into actually being interested. That would be just weird. And a waste of time. You won't need all that stuff later. Even worse, you could ruin your life. You might be too busy studying to keep up with what's going on. You could become a total social outcast. You could even end up doing something silly, like going to medical school or getting an MBA.

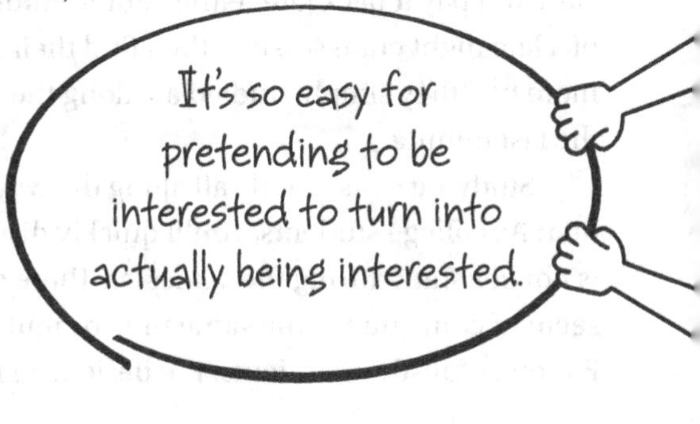
It's so easy for pretending to be interested to turn into actually being interested.

We certainly can't let that happen!

Can we?

John A. Lanning and
Sandra Mizumoto Posey

16. ProcrastiNation

How Not to Be a Citizen

Advice from a Pair of Professors and Administrators . . .

Time management is a major factor for success in college and in life. Just like working out or keeping your hamster cage from smelling like cedar chips and pee, time management requires planning, judgment, and commitment.

Finding the proper time balance between academics, employment, social life, etc. is not easy. What can you do? Establish a routine for time management. Think of all the things in your life that are routine: brushing your teeth (we hope), filling the tank with gas, eating, sleeping, checking your email. If you keep up a time management program for just a month, you will have established lifelong habits that enhance your productivity and put you in charge.

People often view time as a commodity, to be saved, hoarded, and occasionally squandered. You won't, however, find a single ATM that provides time from a checking or savings account. You can't charge time on a credit card and pay it back later either. Some students will try, forgoing sleep in favor of a late night cram session, then find their grades would have improved more had they simply studied all along the way instead of waiting until the last minute.

Studying consistently all along the way may seem counterintuitive at first: As college students, you'll quickly discover that the academic workload is not constant during the semester. There are periods when assignments seem to come due at the same time or multiple tests fall on the same day. For most full-time students, the periods of heightened academic activity occur before midterm, near the drop deadline, and at the end of the semester. While some students may feel this is a diabolical faculty plot, the uneven nature of the academic semester is actually a harbinger of many life cycles beyond college (*and* a diabolical faculty plot). More importantly, it is a pattern that puts additional emphasis on planning and avoiding procrastination.

Two key components to effective time management are setting goals and establishing priorities. Students must clarify their priorities and develop a time management system around their goals. Without goals, the time management ball has nowhere to go. Facebook and other distractions are the other team's goalies. Either kick that ball past them or get rid of the goalies.

Two key components to effective time management are setting goals and establishing priorities.

So what are your goals and priorities? A journal or time log can help you identify how you actually use your time, which is a de facto priorities list. After a week, did you discover the cumulative time you spent texting exceeded the time you spent studying? Bam, I guess you know what your priority is.

Once you've chronicled a week's (or at least a day's) worth of actual time use, start by asking yourself some of these questions:

- What do I spend the majority of time doing? (This will give you a key insight into what your priorities currently really are as opposed to what you think they are)
- What activities are unproductive? (Sad fact: many of these are fun)
- Must all my priorities be academic? (Generally speaking, no. But you need to know which priorities are important when. List *all* your priorities in your journal. Later, you'll reorganize them in order of importance to your long- and short-term goals)
- Have my priorities changed over time? Should they change?

ProcrastiNation, the very real country where most of us live, is the single greatest enemy of effective time management. Here are some tips to help you conquer it:

- Establish both short- and long-range goals:
  - Write down the things that matter to you. These are your priorities. What will matter to you in the future? These are your goals. Refer to your goals often to remind you what is truly important.
  - Be realistic about your goals and expectations of yourself. Don't expect perfection.
  - Break long-range goals into tasks.
  - Check off completed tasks as you do them.
  - Provide yourself with a suitable reward for completed tasks. (After finishing the first chapter of my dissertation, I rewarded myself with jalapeño poppers and an Oreo shake from Jack in the Box. Is this a suitable reward? Only if you want to accomplish the freshman 15—or in my case, the dissertation 15—which refers to how many pounds you'll ultimately gain with these sorts of rewards.)
- Make a prioritized to-do list:
  - List tasks that will help you take steps toward accomplishing your short- and long-range goals.
  - Estimate the time required for each.
  - Set priorities for each task: Which of them do you need to tackle first?
  - A personal planner or calendar, whether paper or electronic, is excellent for establishing and maintaining a prioritized task list.

Don't make the mistake of thinking you can do it all at once. Multitasking is an oft-identified characteristic of this generation. But while eating and reading a biology text simultaneously would appear to save time, texting and driving have serious, and sometimes fatal, consequences. Either way, whether or not you believe the studies that say multitasking is a myth, don't risk your life (or your grades) trying to prove them wrong.

Whatever strategies you use to manage your time, make sure you manage time rather than letting time manage you. Do so successfully and you'll move right on out of ProcrastiNation to Graduation.

Teague von Bohlen

17. Yes, We Can All See You Doing That

It's often been said that a person's real character is what they do when they think nobody's looking. And that's true—or would be, if there were ever a time when no one was looking.

The fact is, people are looking all the time, even when you don't think they are. Maybe especially when you don't think they are. This is the digital age, remember, and Big Brother is everywhere. (George Orwell warned us, but of course, about half of us only read the Cliff's Notes of his book *1984*.)

Of course, if you lock yourself into a small windowless room, you might be safe. (But even then, you should probably check to make sure your webcam isn't on and your phone hasn't butt-dialed anyone.) But if you're in your car? No. Everyone sees you when you're in your car. Everyone's car is like the capital city of nose-picking, singing-out-loud, and generally behaving like an idiot with no social graces whatsoever. Why? Because we have the illusion of invisibility. Or at the very least, the presumption of anonymity. We think that no one can see us, or at least if they do, they don't know us from, well, that other person in traffic. None of it is true, of course, but we believe it. We've all seen people doing gross things in their car, and we've all seen people we know in traffic. It's not unusual. But we pretend that it is.

The same holds true for college. In the classroom, and outside of it too. So yes, your professor is lecturing, but he or she probably isn't so enraptured by the sound of their own voice (they've probably given this lecture a few dozen times by the time you hear it) that they won't notice you digging for nostril gold back there in row 6. Will they stop and admonish you? Of course not. (Well, probably not—I once had an art history professor who did exactly that during a particularly eyelid-heavy session on Botticelli, and she shamed the guy so badly that he dropped the class and never came back . . . which may have been her reason for doing such a thing in the first place, come to think of it.)

And it's not just picking your nose that we're talking about (though I'm focusing on it here because, let's face it, we all learned back in grade school that it was pretty funny). It's anything you might be doing in class that you wouldn't want to admit to doing. The rule of Internet flame wars sort of translates here: If you wouldn't say it to someone's face, don't say it online. Likewise, if you wouldn't do something in full view of your classmates and your profs? Don't do it at all. This includes, but is by no means limited to, sleeping, surfing the web, texting, semi-pornographic doodling, playing massive multiplayer games on your laptop, scratching yourself in tender areas, eating noisily or with gusto, consuming something that might taste great but smells up the joint, or doing the homework for your next class during the lecture for the class you're currently in.

By the way, that last one? It's probably one of your professors' least favorites. It may be the most disrespectful of the bunch, even though it's arguably the most productive in the most strict of senses. Doing work for another course while you're still in someone else's class is tantamount to coming out and saying to a professor "this other class is a lot more important to me than what you're trying to teach me at the moment, and I'm going to prioritize this over what you're working to accomplish now." It sounds harsh, but that's exactly the way it comes across.

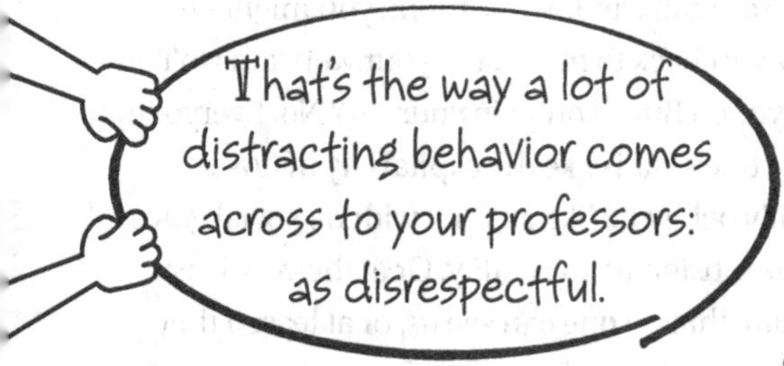
That's the way a lot of distracting behavior comes across to your professors: as disrespectful.

That's the way a lot of distracting behavior comes across to your professors: as disrespectful.

And I can't stress this enough: We always see it. We almost always notice it. Most of us actually write it down in our gradebooks. If it doesn't come out in your participation grade (stuff like this is actually one of the reasons I even have a participation grade!), it'll come out in terms of whether that 89.3 percent remains a B+ or becomes an A−. It all counts.

And like I said earlier, this isn't just about your behavior in the classroom. This is true in meetings with professors and peers, the common room of your dorm, the study area of the school library, or the TV lounge at the student union. Even if you're at a big state school, the pond in which you're swimming is small. Everyone sees everyone, and there's no guarantee of anonymity. In that small pond, you want to be a fish known for something good, something positive. You don't want to be the nose-picking fish, whether that's metaphor or not.

So yeah, character is defined as what you do when no one's looking. Still true. But assume that someone is always watching. Because chances are . . . we are.

Kevin Haworth

18. The Bad Question

Teachers love questions. Really we do. Some teachers will even tell you "there's no such thing as a bad question." And I understand why they would say that. Generally speaking, asking is better than not asking.

When in doubt, go ahead. Raise your hand. Yes, you, right there. Now you're involved in the class. You've gotten started on the road to being an active learner. You're someone who sits forward, stays focused, and follows the conversation. You've also helped me, the professor, know who you are, which is an important step toward consistent success in college classrooms. For these reasons, we might agree that there really is no such thing as a bad question. Right, class? Raise your hand if you agree.

There is such a thing, however, as an *unhelpful* question.

I get asked a lot of unhelpful questions. I always answer these questions, no matter how unhelpful, because I want to encourage my students to gain confidence and stay curious. But at the same time, I try to guide them toward asking more useful questions, the ones that will elicit answers that students really need. Particularly when it comes to writing assignments, I've noticed that students tend to ask very unhelpful questions. I'll introduce a new assignment, usually handing out a prompt on a half-sheet of paper. I'll ask them to take a look at it, and then I'll mention a couple of points to bear in mind while writing. Then I say, "Any questions?" Pause. Students look around. Then a hand goes up.

What follows is almost always an unhelpful question. Well-meaning, but ultimately unhelpful. What makes these questions unhelpful? They don't get you answers—at least not the kind of answers that will help you succeed on the writing assignment you have in front of you. And we want you to succeed—grading those papers is a lot more fun, frankly, when they are well written. So here are some examples of unhelpful questions about your writing assignments, and some suggestions about how you can rephrase them to get the answers you really need.

Question: How long does this paper have to be?

Why It's Unhelpful: Because half the time the professor will respond, "As long as it needs to be," which, let's face it, is about as unhelpful as you can possibly imagine. The other half of the time you'll get the answer, "Five pages, just like it says on the assignment sheet in front of you," which will make you feel, well, kinda embarrassed. (It doesn't feel good for the professor either; we would rather you read the assignment sheet carefully.)

Better Version: What are some of the things that I need to accomplish in this assignment?

When students ask how long a paper has to be, they are really trying to figure out what kind of points they need to touch on, how many, and how in depth their exploration needs to be. They do a kind of mental calculus in which they try to determine the answers to these questions based on paper length, which is like trying to measure the size of an elephant's heart by looking at its skin. The better version of this question gets you right into the thinking process, and can prompt even more helpful questions. For example, if the professor answers, "You need to make a persuasive argument," you can follow that with, "Can you say more about what a good persuasive argument looks like?" The best questions start a conversation, not finish it.

Question: Is it okay if I write about ________?

Why It's Unhelpful: College professors aren't elementary school teachers. We don't like questions that remind us of "Is it OK if I visit the bathroom?" In fact, we try to get you out of the habit of asking permission, and into the habit of asserting your interests. Good writing comes out of being interested and engaged in your subject, though it makes sense to check if your interests and the goals of the writing assignment overlap.

Better Version: I'm interested in ________. How well does that fit the writing assignment?

The first step is to state your interest affirmatively and with confidence. That shows that you're invested in what you're saying. Then, follow that with an open-ended phrase such as "how well does this fit?" or "how appropriate is this topic?" That invites the professor to assess your interests in light of the assignment, and to help you figure out ways to make your interests and the writing assignment work together. You may have to tweak your original idea, but now you've helped the professor become invested in what you want to explore.

Question: Is ________ a good idea?

Why It's Unhelpful: Like the "is it OK" question, this question is unhelpful because it basically calls for a yes or no response—and either way, you're not getting much information. But more importantly, college professors aren't really in the business of judging your ideas as good or bad. We're in the business of helping you *express* your ideas efficiently, fluently, and with sufficient evidence. The brilliant writer and excellent professor David Foster Wallace wrote in one of his syllabi, "I draw no distinction between the quality of one's ideas and the quality of those ideas' verbal expression." In other words, there's no such thing as a good idea in theory—only one that is supported by good writing on the page.

Better Version: See above. State your idea with confidence. Then ask about the best ways to explore it in the context of the assignment.

Question: Is this a research paper? Or is it, like, just my opinion?

Why It's Unhelpful: Students always seem to put the word "just" in front of "opinion," which indicates a sense that formulating opinions involves less work than doing research. That shouldn't be the case. But like the page-length question, you're not asking what you really need to know.

Better Version: For this assignment, what kinds of evidence do I need to support my claims?

Most, if not all, writing assignments involve making claims (what students will often call "their ideas," or "their points" or even "their opinions") and supporting those claims with evidence. But different assignments demand different kinds of evidence. Evidence can be as

Most, if not all, writing assignments involve making claims and supporting those claims with evidence.

numbers-based as statistics ("this activity is dangerous because it carries a 10 percent mortality rate") or as personal as your own life history ("this activity feels dangerous to me because I've seen people get hurt doing this"). It can involve quoting texts you've read for class, or going out in the world and making observations of your own. Oftentimes, you'll draw on several different kinds of evidence to support your claims. Asking the professor what kind of evidence he or she expects to see is exactly the kind of question that will help you succeed in the assignment.

Students often imagine that college classes are about answers—receiving information in the form of professors' lectures or reading that you do for class. But college is just as much about learning how to ask questions. Asking useful questions is a skill, and like any skill it takes practice and some effort to break old habits. But putting in the time is worth it. Otherwise, if you ask yourself that most basic question, *"Will I get an A on this paper?,"* the answer is likely to be no.

Sandra Mizumoto Posey

19. Bring Me Your Tired, Your Hungry, Your Mediocre, Yearning for Grade C

Advice from a Professor and Administrator . . .

Shhh. I'm going to tell you a secret: The usual reason students fail my course is that they simply failed to turn something (or many somethings) in.

That's it. Sometimes they were less-than-stellar class participants, and sometimes their writing wasn't the best or their logic was flawed, but that alone wouldn't usually fail them. To fail, they pretty much had to *fail to turn something in entirely*. Even otherwise excellent writers and class participants sometimes make this mistake and they fail too, much to my and their chagrin.

Your takeaway from this? Turn it in. Even if your paper is less than stellar, even with a failing grade on that on that single assignment, it would probably add up to at least 50 percent of whatever overall percent of your grade it represents. Don't turn it in and you'll lose that 50 percent, turning its value into 100 percent loss.

Your takeaway from this? Turn it in.

Wait. Did that make any sense? Listen, I never claimed to be a mathematician; I'm a folklorist for goodness sake, but I do know that even a failing assignment would receive *some* points, whereas a missing assignment will receive zero points. Some hurts less than zero when the final tabulation comes around. No one really cares in the long run what you got on that quiz or midterm. Fail to show up for the quiz or midterm though and you're risking affecting your overall class grade and people *will* care about that.

So show up. Be mediocre if you have to because some other class is kicking your ass. Be mediocre because this is general studies and you could really care less about my class. Be mediocre because you partied, stayed up all night, and just didn't have time to do the reading. Mediocre might still get you a C, no matter how much I want to fail you, because when I tally up all the assignments, lo and behold, you turned every mediocre one in.

Mind you, if you explicitly don't follow directions, maybe even argue with me about the directions in the paper itself (yes, this has happened) and do the exact opposite of what I ask, I may just give you a zero on that assignment. But if you make a fair effort, I can't give you zero. Then, if all the stars align in your favor on that final tallying day, chances are you will get a C.

Want to accomplish this without simply hoping for the stars to align? Then you do the math. It's all there on your syllabus: Your syllabus tells you which assignments count for what percent. As the grades start flowing in, you'll know just how well you have to do on the final to save yourself from that low grade you got on the midterm. But if you failed to turn in that first paper or failed to show up for the midterm, that final hurdle to a passing grade may well be insurmountable.

So it's OK. Your paper kind of sucks. It will make your professor wince and rue the day you entered their classroom. But you'll get a few points for it, and a few points are better than no points. Point taken?

20. The "Do-I-Know-You?" Grade

For some professors, your final letter grade is a strict representation of your calculated scores, regardless of how fractionally close you are to the next letter grade. For other professors, though, if you are on the cusp of the better grade, it gives them pause.

This is a good thing for you; that's when a professor might consider your "do I know you?" grade to decide your final grade for the course.

Your "do I know you?" grade is a subjective rating, based on your professor's memory of your level of involvement in and contribution to the class. This "do I know you?" grade can be the difference between receiving the more generous grade on the better side of the plus or minus, or just staying put at the calculated grade that was right on the edge. Sometimes that small change in grade makes all the difference in the world to a student's GPA.

Say your professor is at the end of a long semester (yes, they're long for your professors too), and your professor comes across your grade. Your raw score is a 79.2. On the plus side, you passed. On the not-so-plus side, you're eight-tenths of a percentage point from a B−, as opposed to a C+. That can make a big difference, from the psychological to the practical. Your professor might well consider your "do I know you?" grade. Did you attend every class? Did you pay attention? Were you respectful and considerate toward your classmates? Did you ask questions in class when you needed clarity? Did you visit during office hours when you needed help? The answers to each of these questions and a few others are going to determine whether your final grade is C level or higher.

Important stuff, right? Fortunately, you can have a positive impact on your "do I know you?" grade by following four simple rules. (Warning: You can just as easily tank your "do I know you?" grade by ignoring these same rules.)

Rule 1: Show Up

You have to attend every class meeting. Not only does showing up put you in position to learn what is being taught, it also gives you face time with the professor. When your professors determine your "do I know you?" grades, the first thing they'll ask themselves is this: Do I know who this is? Your professor will note whether you are memorable for attending class or missing it, and whether they know you for your punctuality or your tardiness.

Rule 2: Pay Attention

When you are in class, you are there to learn. Your tuition affords you the privilege of being in that course with that professor on that campus. Make sure you get your money's worth. That means fully participating in the experience of the course. Anything other than providing your full attention to the learning that is taking place would detract from that experience and would be distracting for you, your classmates, and ultimately your professor. That means stay off your iPhone and Facebook, and make sure that your professor "catches" you paying attention at least once per lecture. Eye contact makes a difference.

When you are in class, you are there to learn.

Rule 3: Be Engaged

The best way to be known by your professor is to ask thoughtful, curious questions and to offer insightful observations and comments. While in class, raise your hand and engage. Ask or answer questions. You may be helping your classmates understand a concept and assisting your professor with clarifying a point. If you don't receive a complete understanding after asking for explanations in class, approach your professor directly after class. If your confusion occurs outside of class meeting times, visit or call your professor during office hours or send an email. Also, if you occasionally read an article or watch a video directly related to a topic recently covered in class, share it with your professor; it makes a good impression. Regardless, when initiating any sort of contact with your professors, make sure your approach is intentional, respectful, and appropriate.

Rule 4: Do Your Best

The primary contributors to your "do I know you?" grade are your grades themselves. Usually, if a professor is assessing your "do I know you?" grade it is because you did not receive the best scores in the class. The professor will look to see what you earned on your assignments and why. Not fully grasping the concepts or making common mistakes is one thing; poor grammar, carelessness, not following directions, not fully contributing on group projects, or not even trying is quite another. If you get a mediocre grade on your exam, but throw yourself into truly understanding the content you didn't master during the exam, you're setting yourself up for a generous nod in the case of the "do I know you?" grade.

Clearly, these tips aren't rocket science (even if you are, in fact, studying rocket science). But curiously, they're not only the best method of getting a grade-bump if you end up on the cusp, but also the best method of getting better grades in the first place.

So there it is, the inner workings of the "do I know you?" grade. The nuances of how the grade is developed and applied may seem somewhat nebulous, but one thing should be clear: You, and only you, are in control of how you fare with this portion of your grade. Just remember, all you have to do is show up, pay attention, be engaged, and do your best. This is *your* education; *you* have to own it.

Sandra Mizumoto Posey

21. B.S. Is a Path to Truth

Advice from a Professor and Administrator...

"B.S. is a path to truth."

That's what I shared on day one with my first year Honor's class in Interdisciplinary General Education 120: Consciousness and Community. I figured they could handle it. Sure, we also read educational revolutionaries like Paulo Freire and bell hooks. We read ancient and modern literary works from *Gilgamesh* to *A Raisin in the Sun*. But over the course of the quarter, we revisited that concept, "B.S. is a path to truth," over and over again from different angles until they understood that it was more than their professor trying to be irreverent and funny (which, OK, she was). It was the gosh darn, honest, profound secret to life: B.S. **is** a path to truth. In fact, it may be **the** path the truth.

This is not to say you should B.S. your professor about why you are late to class or why you have to leave early. You shouldn't B.S. about why your assignment is late, short, or never came in. Saying that your printer isn't working—that's always B.S., so don't even go there. No, B.S., gentle reader, is bigger than that, more important than that, and deserves better than that. B.S. is the key to the humanities.

What are the humanities anyway? I doubt you'll get any given pair of humanities scholars to agree on what the heck it is, but more or less it is about what it is that makes us all human. And what is it that makes us all human? B.S. makes us human. And that's why the humanities, more than science or social science, are truer and more important than other academic disciplines. It's just closer to the truth: B.S. makes us human, B.S. makes us brilliant, B.S. makes us who we are and *what we can be.* And even if you are determined to be a scientist and use the scientific method to verify and cross-verify all your findings, you'll never get to be a good scientist without a heavy dose of honest-to-goodness B.S.

Somewhere or another that god-awful internal critic that tells you that you don't know how to think and you don't know how to write and you don't know what the author meant turns off.

Think about it: What were the best papers you ever wrote for a class? Probably the ones for which you stayed up all night, drinking too much coffee, and the information from the texts you were reading were but a blur in front of your eyes and in your brain. But the paper was due at 8 a.m. the next day, and you had to turn something in. So you wrote and wrote and wrote. Heck, you don't even remember all of what you wrote. Somewhere or another that god-awful internal critic that tells you that you don't know how to think and you don't know how to write and you don't know what the author meant turns off. And your right brain takes over. You write, you write, you write.

The next day you turned it in. You probably should have proofread the thing—twice. If you had, you may have even gotten an A. You could have found the kernels of truth your right brain had been spewing out like a dam bursting forth—your right brain struggles so often under the dull nagging of your left brain telling you that you aren't good enough. When it finally gets the chance to be free of that, your right brain will go crazy with abandon and glee.

Left brain, though, is good the next morning for editing. Left brain would have caught the fact that you used *their* instead of *they're* or, that perennial favorite, that you used *defiantly* instead of *definitely*. (Don't rely on spell-check. Spellcheck is even more left brain than left brain and the two of them together will leave you in B grade hell.)

The genius of your right brain though, might charm your professor to the extent that you may have lucked out and gotten an A—much to you and your cynic left-brain's surprise. If you did, it was through the right-brain's defiance, definitely. The genius of your right brain, with enough coffee in the morning, may have danced you deftly through the *their/they're* straits. Either way, the point is, B.S. is the path to setting your genius right brain free. And when your right brain dances free, you may realize it holds insights into Freire, hooks, or whoever, when you didn't even realize it *understood* them.

For now, it's 6 a.m. That paper is due in two hours. Wake your left brain the hell up and tell it to read that paper over, twice. Don't let left brain be seduced by right brain's charm—that's it's weakness. They fell for each other once and have never really parted. Give that paper a good, long edit. Get your roommate's left brain to look at it too. (Your roommate doesn't have the history your own right and left brain do and is likely to be a little more objective.) Now get some more coffee. Be on time for class. Don't B.S. about being late. Take a deep, cold breath of morning air and tell the right brain it's about to dance again during class discussion. Remind it, though, to listen too. There are other people dancing, and while dancing alone is fun, dancing together is ecstatic.

Teague von Bohlen and
Sandra Mizumoto Posey

22. Great Writers Steal . . . But Not Like That

Advice from a Pair of Professors . . .

The original quote is from T.S. Eliot, though it's been misattributed to everyone from Oscar Wilde to Mark Twain to Picasso, and then some. It been popularly paraphrased thusly: "Good writers borrow; great writers steal."

It sounds like a defense of plagiarism, doesn't it? Yeah, well, it's not. And please don't try to use it to defend such academic crimes, because it won't work, and it will get you a long lecture on Eliot, the constructive and conscious borrowing of situation and theme, and questionable ethics, none of which will get you off the punitive hook for essentially stealing someone else's work.

That's right: stealing. Plagiarism is intellectual and artistic theft. And we have enough of that in the world (thank you, Internet).

On our syllabi, like most professors, we're required to have a stated policy about plagiarism. Plagiarism, as you know, is the use of another writers' wording or phrasing without giving that person credit for having written it first. You know: the way you used to write reports back in middle school.

But like almost everything else that worked for you back in middle school, plagiarism just hasn't stood the test of time. If you did it in high school and got away with it, you were lucky. If you do it in college, you just won't get away with it, for several reasons. For one thing, it's incredibly easy for any writing professor (or even a science prof who pays attention to style as well as substance) to recognize when you're writing in your voice, and when you're borrowing from someone or somewhere else. This has always been the standby for identifying cheaters like this—personal experience. This is also how a lot of students got away with it here and there, even if in the end (it's true), they only cheated themselves. (Ah, the great cliché. Also true, but only if you mature past eighth grade. If you plan on sticking to the emotional development of middle school for the remainder of your natural life, you're golden—but then why are you reading this book?)

More importantly, in today's digital age, it's nearly impossible to find a good source for something to copy that's not already searchable on the web. All a professor has to do to check to see whether you've plagiarized is to plug a sentence or phrase into a search engine, and *voila*: You're hosed.

Fortunately, there's a way to avoid this: just do the work. When you pull text from another source, quote it. Cite it using the standard for that discipline. Then elaborate in *your own words.* Trust your own words. College is about finding your own voice and you'll never do that if you don't use it. Plus, there's a benefit for actually doing the work. You improve yourself and your understanding of the material. That critical paper you didn't cheat on? Might just help you on the essay portion of the final exam.

And tests? For gosh sakes, don't cheat. Trust us, you're just not as subtle as you think you are.

Here's the thing: Cheating of any stripe is grounds for failing the course in question, and possibly expulsion from the university (which we guarantee will look bad on your résumé). The risk is completely out of scale with the possible reward. Not having to think a little bit, and spend a bit of time writing a few paragraphs on your own, versus possibly losing your opportunity to attend the college of your choice (or maybe one at all)? Bad trade.

And here's the thing: If you're reading this, there's a good chance that you're already on a good road already, toward something honorable and success-laden and happy. People are already proud of you for getting where you are. You're proud of yourself too, and you should be.

Don't jeopardize that just because eating ramen and watching *Judge Judy* sounds like more fun in the moment.

section three

Beyond Class

"Was the interview too early for you?"

Andrewgenn/Fotolia

Patricia Colleen Murphy

23. Will Work for Free

Campus Publications and You

Advice from a Professor . . .

Maybe you were editor-in-chief of your high school newspaper/yearbook/literary magazine. So was I. So were about 500 of the first-year students at your new university.

Now that you're in the big leagues, you're probably trying to decide whether working for a campus publication is how you want to spend your precious extracurricular hours.

If you're an English or journalism or communications major, the campus publication is an obvious choice. Working on a university publication gives you a good résumé line, it helps get you involved and knowledgeable about your college community, and it also teaches you hands-on skills that you can describe in a job interview. When I was writing for my college paper, I got to cover stories on local comedy clubs, campus concerts, and nearby restaurants. Each topic I covered got me out of my dorm room and meeting new people; plus the expenses were often comped or reimbursed—quite the boon for a starving student.

But please note that you're starting from scratch now, which will most likely mean that you'll go from making final editorial decisions to being a beat reporter. Please also note that these positions can Suck. You. Dry.

I've seen it happen. I'm the founding editor of a national literary magazine run entirely by undergraduate students. My interns earn three hours of upper-division English credit in exchange for working 150 hours a semester on the magazine. The internship is conducted all online, so the students can complete the work from home or abroad. This cuts down some of the travel time that other internships carry. But it can also make it harder for students to get motivated to do the work.

I require my interns to track their weekly hours in a spreadsheet, and I work hard to encourage them to stay on top of tasks. But not every student is cut out for the discipline and effort it takes to be an unpaid intern. One of my recent interns worked for my literary magazine and the university newspaper during the same semester. She had a very hard time keeping up with the assignments and she had many sleepless nights trying to do both jobs.

Overextending is just one of the many concerns you should think about before devoting your heart and soul to someone else's publication. Really, there are serious pros and cons here, people. Let's take a look at some of the biggies.

Overextending is just one of the many concerns you should think about before devoting your heart and soul to someone else's publication.

The Cons

- **Utter and abject lack of time.** Remember in 4th grade when you were assigned the task of making a diorama depicting a scene from your favorite book? I do. And I remember it because I thought it would take me an hour and it took me about 25. That's what very often happens with the creative process and with the publication process as well. A task you think will be a breeze takes forever as you wait for a call back for an interview or for an email with art to go with your story. You may work so hard on a campus publication that your other schoolwork suffers.
- **You're working for free.** Some campus publications pay a small stipend or offer college credit. But it all boils down to this. You'll be doing a lot of hard work that other people, in grown-up jobs, get paid a lot more to do. A campus publication is essentially a nonprofit organization. You'll be assigned some tasks that seem pointless and ridiculous, such as color-coordinating the pencils. Said tasks would be just fine, if you were salaried and had health benefits. But when you're an intern you might resent them. So beware the trap of committing to a project with no promise of payment, except for smiles.
- **Lack of planning on your part does not constitute an emergency on my part.** Work on campus publications can be highly charged and stressful. Since you're always working with deadlines, someone is going to want you to finish something when they want you to finish it. While your personal priority might be to cram for a French quiz, your editor's priority is to get the publication to press on time. Note that missed deadlines happen, and whether you're the one who missed the deadline or the one who did not receive what you needed on time, working in a deadline-driven workplace can be a stressful march toward disappointment.

The Pros

- **Learning time management.** Nothing will be more important to your future than your ability to manage your time. We're talking about a life skill that affects every moment, waking and sleeping. If you procrastinate that article and wait until 2 a.m. to start it, every part of your life shifts. You will lack sleep, your relationships will suffer, the quality of your work will decrease, and you'll cause yourself massive anxiety. Working for a campus publication helps you realize how one event is intrinsically linked to another. You'll get practice in gettin'er done.
- **Improving writing skills.** I'm going to lay it all out there and assert that the second most important part of your future is your ability to write well. That may seem like an overstatement, but let me tell you why I believe it's true. Unless you learn to communicate fluidly and easily through writing, you will dread any job you enter. Every job requires writing. And the only way to become a better writer is to write. Working on a campus publication gives you a lot of practice.
- **Reducing time available to get into trouble.** College is fun. You're part of a vibrant community full of beautiful young people who like to hang out and, I don't know, play tag football on the quad. Or not. College students seek out lots of different ways to connect with others. Some of those connections tend to involve trouble. Campus publications do not. You'll meet people who are united toward a common goal. You'll spend time with smart peers. You might even hang out after hours. But the objective is clear and pure: putting out the best writing possible.

Campus publications (and many other on-campus job opportunities) have plenty of spaces for students who are willing to learn and who are willing to work. Several of my former interns have gone on to get scholarships to graduate school, get jobs in editing and publishing, and start their own businesses. They succeeded because they were smart enough to know that experience **is** payment. So even if you're not getting that cold hard cash, a strong reference letter is worth its weight in gold.

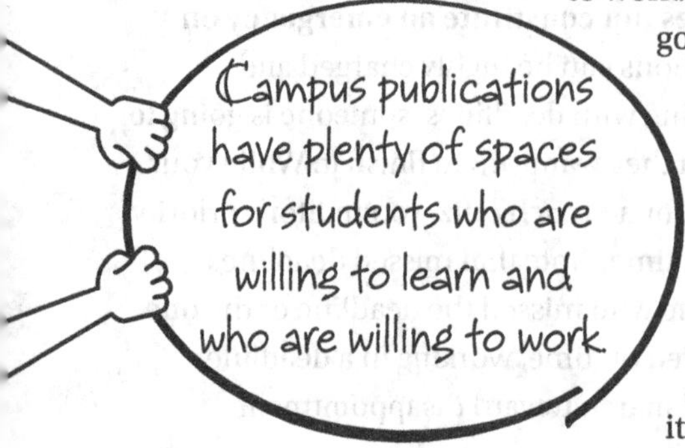
Campus publications have plenty of spaces for students who are willing to learn and who are willing to work.

Bryan Smith

24. Volunteer Work? No Way . . . Pay Me

Advice from a Student . . .

Being a college student has few financial advantages outside of discounted movie tickets and reduced bus fare. What's worse, being a student also slaps a sign on your forehead that reads "will work for free."

I'm here to tell you: If you volunteer, you're a sucker.

The truth is, even as a college student, your work is worth money. But there's a huge educational infrastructure that will work to convince you otherwise. Student groups work largely off of volunteerism. Even commercial companies in the community will lure you in with internships that pay you in experience, life lessons, and a whole slew of other intangibles that, no matter how good they might be for your soul, won't do anything to pay your rent. If you want to start making cold hard cash in college—simply do it. The opportunity is out there to have collegiate financial stability if you look for it and work hard enough.

When I was a freshman, I was dead set on finding a place to work for the long haul of academia. I fulfilled that goal by working at the campus rec. center and the student newspaper. It was only my second week of school when I walked into the newspaper office with my résumé, a portfolio of writing samples, and a little bit of (sort of false) confidence. The editor-in-chief at the time interviewed me and gave me a writing assignment on the spot. I wrote my first draft over the weekend and it was official—I was an employed writer. I didn't have to go through an arduous three months of interning to a maybe-possibly-sorta-kinda shot at getting paid real money.

To phrase it modestly: My story is really a meteoric rise to prominence. OK, not really. But sometimes putting all of your eggs in one basket works—you just have to make sure it's the right basket. Journalism is something I had a passion for starting in high school. Naturally, I jumped on the opportunity to be paid to practice my craft, and that paid off—literally. I worked my way up from freelancer to staff writer to section editor, and finally to editor-in-chief, running the whole thing. Had I not started early and led myself with the mentality that my work was worth much more than just gaining experience, I probably wouldn't have stuck around for five years.

Here's the thing: Before you can convince the outside world that you're worth a paycheck, you have to believe it yourself. So when you want something, show up and ask for it. And don't show up empty handed. Bring a résumé and samples of your work. Bring something that shows potential employers that you care about cultivating your talents and you're not screwing around. When they offer you that initial student-type, unpaid gig, tell them (in a professional tone, of course), "No way . . . pay me."

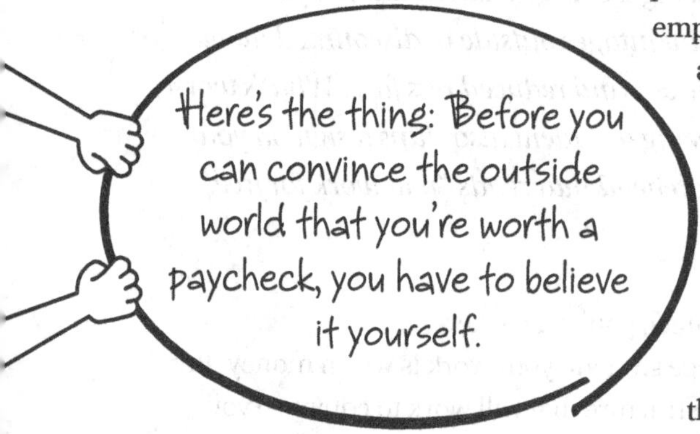
Here's the thing: Before you can convince the outside world that you're worth a paycheck, you have to believe it yourself.

Sure, there's merit in volunteering your time and soaking in professional experience for 25 hours every week. But once you start digging that hole, it's difficult to climb out of it. And then you run the risk of being sucked into the vacuum of working for free even in the postacademic realm. Having line after line of experience on your résumé will dazzle employers, no doubt. But when you've got that experience *and* a salary history to back it up—they'll be looking for ways to add your name to their roster.

The college experience is definitely worth something. Practical experience and learning on the job are worth even more. But making enough to pay down some of your credit cards while getting that education? Priceless.

Patricia Colleen Murphy

25. To Friend or Not to Friend

Social Networking and Your Professors

Advice from a Professor . . .

One summer I hired a student to write a series of blog posts for my magazine. The student's performance was spotty. Sometimes the completed blog posts showed up in my inbox on time and sometimes they did not. But what did show up, like clockwork, were the student's drunken and X-rated Tweets on my Twitter feed every evening at cocktail hour.

Let's just say the relationship did not end with a glowing letter of recommendation.

Truth is, for first-year college students reading this essay, by the time you've graduated and entered the job market, the world of social networking will be remarkably different than it is now. Still, you have the next four years to read, study, make friends, and basically have the time of your life. Odds are you're likely to share some of those moments on Facebook, Google+, Twitter, Tumblr, Instagram, or Pinterest. If you're going to be sharing anyway, why not use those social networking hours toward a greater good? I'm assuming you'd like to get good grades in college and then get a job or go to grad school after you graduate, right? Believe it or not, social networking can help you.

Just as your 20-something friends are likely to be on Facebook, so are your 40-something professors. And chances are they are friends with other people in their fields who are writing articles, winning grants, and hiring for jobs. This creates a deep network of connections that can offer insight into the subjects you are studying in class and the jobs surrounding those subjects. Widening your social networks to include more professionals means you become more professional.

Another benefit of engaging with your professors on social networks is that you can understand more about what they want from their students in class. You can interact with them online in thoughtful and careful ways that will make you stand out above other classmates. And depending on what you post, your professors will gain (or lose) a great deal of respect for you. You might even think of your social networking as extra credit—use your networks to further examine issues you're discussing in your coursework, and your professors will see that you are sincere and ready to learn. Professors also sometimes post about their lives as teachers and scholars, which will help you understand why they make the choices they make.

But even beyond your college career, know that your next boss will Google you. Therefore it's to your benefit to start developing your online professional presence now. No matter what field you enter, you'll set yourself up for success if you leave evidence of your self-discipline, intellect, and social engagement on the web. Think of all of your online accounts as being a portfolio available to a future employer. It's important to follow several steps to put your best gigabyte forward. Here's how.

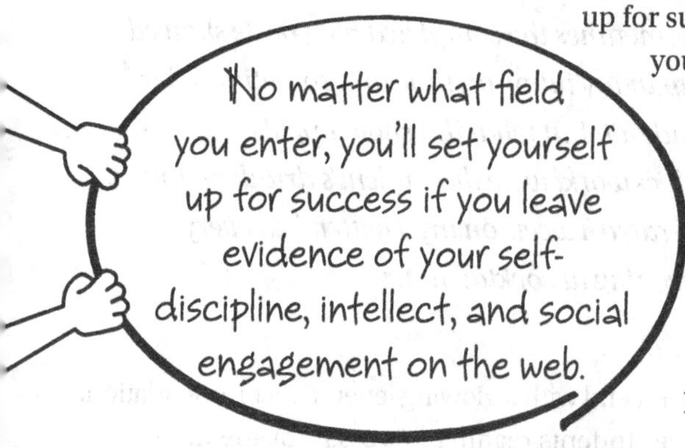
No matter what field you enter, you'll set yourself up for success if you leave evidence of your self-discipline, intellect, and social engagement on the web.

Do

1. **Do create an online brand.** First, take down any photos or posts that are not appropriate. You want to make sure that the first thing a prof or boss sees represents a positive image of you as a human being. Post more pics from your work on a Habitat for Humanity build and delete the ones from the raging kegger. Get a professional headshot and use it as your profile picture across networks. Pick a topic you're passionate about (besides beer), and make sure 80 percent of your posts to social networks are on point. Avoid topics like politics and religion, and stay instead with academic subjects or special hobbies and interests. Read articles about your specific topics and share them on your networks. This shows that you are motivated, informed, and focused: three very attractive qualities in both students and employees.

2. **Do grow your network.** What do you see when you read your Facebook feed? The posts you see are only as good as the people you friend. Even if you use your Facebook account to communicate with your family members and close buddies, you can also use it to enter a community of people in your field. Majoring in mathematics? Why not friend the author of your textbook, then friend their friends so that you now have a feed filled with experts? Now, instead of posts about someone's new boots or bad case of sniffles, you'll get posts about publications, conferences, and jobs in your professional area. The same is true with Google+, Twitter, and LinkedIn. You can control the information you receive by carefully choosing your networks and circles.
3. **Do use social networking, not social narcissism.** Social networks are a great way to share information with a lot of people in a short amount of time. This can be a great thing, or a truly terrible one. We all have that Facebook friend who can't resist posting every random thought that comes to mind, along with blurry and/or inappropriate smartphone pics. But when we stop to think about the word *Network,* what really comes to mind is "connection." It's time to think of the goal of social networking as a way to connect with others. Instead of dumping information onto your own profiles, you should engage in thoughtful conversations with other people. Make it a goal to spend more time giving than receiving.
4. **Do create an interactive resume.** You're smart. You're tech savvy. You're going to spend the next four years becoming an expert in something. So why not create a website that focuses on your accomplishments? Go to Wordpress.com and sign up for a website. It will take you 10 minutes, tops. Pick a URL that matches your learning and career goals and that would be interesting and attractive to an employer. Write some blog posts about your goals. Create a page that is your résumé. Don't have anything to put on your résumé? Then get to work. Go to the career services center at your campus and ask to see a strong sample. Then seek out activities that you can fill into those blank spots. Not only will this help you keep track of what you have done, it will also help you decide what to do next. Light on community service? Join a spring break volunteer trip. Light on work experience? Take an internship with a local nonprofit agency. No matter what, keep your résumé site professional, focused, and updated so that it works as a living portfolio of your interests and accomplishments.

Don't

1. **Don't play Farmville.** Or any other games. Not on this account, anyway.
2. **Don't "like" anything that you wouldn't talk about in front of your grandma.** Seriously.
3. **Don't post sexy photos.** Or talk about how you really miss dropping acid before going to shows. Again: respect the grandma rule.
4. **Don't reveal anything about yourself that you'd be afraid to talk about in your next big job interview.** Because for better or for worse, that's exactly what you're doing in posting things online under your real name.

Bottom line. Would you walk into math class naked? Would you disrespect women in front of your mother? Would you show up drunk to a job? If the answer is no, then step away from your smartphone.

Mindy Bezdek

26. Choose Your Own Adventure

Taking Advantage of Student Travel

Universities have huge egos. They believe that they're the end-all, be-all of learning, like they are all that and a bag of academic chips. But despite what universities may like you to think, not all education takes place within their hallowed halls.

There's a whole world out there. It's all fine and good to sit in a classroom and see different cultures from the perspective of the textbook and your professor; both have valuable things to teach you, but you're not getting the whole picture. You're getting the flat, 2-D version of someone else's vision. To really understand the world, you've got to get out of that ivory tower (or even that community college!) and see it for yourself.

That's what I did, and I've never regretted it. Some people might think that taking time to travel is wasting time better spent driving full-steam toward a degree—but in my experience, it's just the opposite. My travels have done nothing but enhance my education.

There is no doubt that it is way more fun to wander the world than it is to sit in a classroom. Much of what you learn on the road is absorbed effortlessly and stays with you permanently—for better or for worse. And you learn things you never knew you didn't know. Just a few of the lessons I've learned in my travels: Aboriginal dreamtime stories often acted as maps; a Communist group called the Shining Path tried to overthrow the Peruvian government in the 1980s; Tasmanian devils are ridiculously cute, but they have a blood curdling snarl that clearly was the inspiration for them being called *devil*.

A lot of what will make an impression on you isn't what you'd expect. Sure, Machu Picchu is amazing, Uluru (Ayer's Rock) leaves you feeling spiritually touched, and Bangkok is insane; but everyone knows that. It is, of course, awesome to experience it for yourself, but this is the same basic stuff you can learn from a book. What you can't experience in a traditional classroom setting are the things and people you never expected to encounter. These experiences may seem unusual—and they often are—but they also signal some of the things we all have in common.

And it's not just the people you meet on your travels that may take you by surprise. You yourself will probably become more spontaneous—you lose your routines, your habits, and the expectations that others place on you. When you travel, especially if you're on your own, you are completely and absolutely free. Other than obeying the laws of the land (which you have to do—you don't want to experience the legal systems of other lands, after all), you can do whatever you want, whenever you want. You won't have that sort of freedom in your "regular" life, maybe ever.

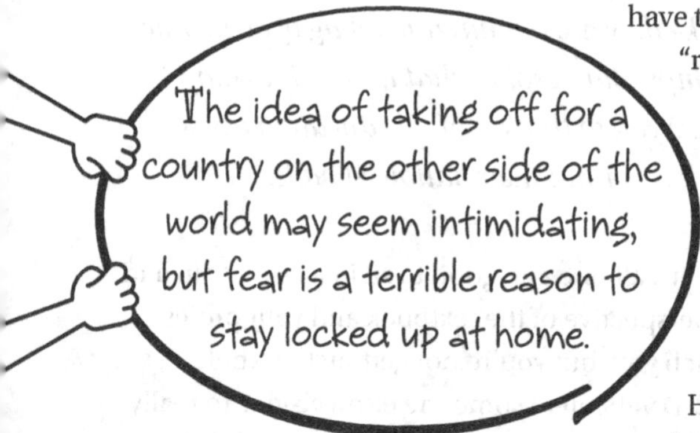
The idea of taking off for a country on the other side of the world may seem intimidating, but fear is a terrible reason to stay locked up at home.

The idea of taking off for a country on the other side of the world may seem intimidating, but fear is a terrible reason to stay locked up at home. There are dangers, but usually they can be avoided. Here are a few tips for traveling safely and constructively as a student.

1. **Always do your research.** Scammers and con men aren't usually creative; these uninspired bad guys use the same tricks over and over on tourists. Most towns have their own easily discovered scams. For example, taxi drivers in Mexico City can be dangerous; the wrong one may try to kidnap you. To avoid this, you should only take taxis that you have called yourself. And some of the risks are less about safety and more about usury: In Bangkok, some tuk-tuk drivers (like taxi drivers) will offer you a tour of the city for the equivalent of 25 cents. What they will actually give you is a tour of all the shops that have paid those drivers to bring in tourists.
2. **Use your common sense.** Don't walk around with large amounts of money bulging out of your pocket. Leave your passport locked up at the hotel. Don't look lost. (And if you are lost, fake it until you find your way.)
3. **Trust your instincts.** Most cities don't have wandering good Samaritans who offer advice to tourists. If someone you meet is being unusually nice, if you feel like you're being followed, or if anything feels strange at all, pay

attention to that and *react*. That might mean going into a café or just flat-out telling someone you are not interested. Most scammers are only interested in your money, and if you're not the easy mark they were hoping for, they know another will be along anytime.

4. **Take in the small things.** Pay attention to where you are at all times—not just because it makes you more safe (it does), but also because if you're dozing off, you'll miss the local stuff that shows not only the culture of the place in which you find yourself, but also the people that inhabit it. You'll want to remember that friendly, hilarious, and somewhat pushy salesman from the bus ride—the one trying to sell everyone a seemingly magical potion that cures everything from cancer to colds and makes you super attractive to the opposite sex and smell great besides. But you won't have the chance if you aren't enjoying the moments between the moments.
5. **Choose the more interesting path.** Most of the lessons that you'll treasure from these experiences aren't afternoons in museums. You can wake up in one town and decide that its food is terrible and its dogs are unfriendly, and hop on a bus that same afternoon. Instead of seeing yet another piece of (admittedly awesome) art, you can spend an entire day watching a leashed cow try to escape a farmer by swimming down a river. Everything is possible; all things are on the menu. Don't limit yourself to the things that every other tourist "just has to see."

Seeing the world isn't about finding yourself (you know where you are) and it probably won't lead you directly to a career (that's what college is for), but it will open your mind to different perspectives. What traveling will do is help you appreciate and take advantage of your education and your life. It is hard to know what you have when you're surrounded by people that have the similar things, and it's hard to understand your own culture until you see it from an outside perspective.

And, of course, the main reason to get out into the world is that traveling is fun. Don't become one of those people who say, "I wish I would have traveled when I was young." Those people are sad. You want to be one of those people with the stories that their friends love to hear about . . . and you will be. So long as you avoid the cabs in Mexico City.

And, of course, the main reason to get out into the world is that traveling is fun.

Teague von Bohlen

27. Learning to Walk

What You Need to Know about Graduation Ceremonies

Advice from a Professor . . .

You'd think, after all the learning that you've done over the last four odd years (or five, or six), you'd be ready for the pomp and circumstance that caps (and gowns) it all. But listen up, because this is important: you're so *not.*

Everyone—I mean everyone—is surprised by all the stuff that they have to do when it comes to actually registering for graduation. (Yes, there's your first surprise: You have to register.) Students seem to think that graduation just sort of . . . happens. And it sort of did, back in high school, when students are more or less taken care of, either by their parents or their school or both. But like all the other aspects of college, which you will have by then figured out is all up to you, so is graduation.

The first thing you need to do to prep for graduation happens long before you're done with your academics: See your advisor. Many times—at least once per academic year. And not just your core advisor, who'll be responsible for making sure that you've satisfied all the requirements of a bachelor's degree in whatever. You also want to talk with your major advisor (you should have one of these—or, if not, someone in the department through which you're taking your major should be able to talk with you and advise, if only unofficially) about whether you've completed everything you need to complete to actually, you know, graduate with a degree in a specific discipline.

One of my duties as an English professor at my institution of higher learning used to be advising majors, and I can tell you that most of the students I spoke with were very confused about what they needed to take, and in what order, and whether they needed to pass with a specific minimum grade in those required courses in order to count toward graduation. (To answer that last question? Yes. At many institutions, for a course to count in your major, you'll need to not only pass them, but to earn a grade of C or better. No, a C– doesn't cut it.) Many of them had taken too many classes of one type (writing courses, for my majors), and some of them wouldn't count. Poor planning (and sometimes poor advising) is one of the reasons that some students don't graduate in four years. And while the five-year plan isn't the end of the world, it costs a lot more money, and it's a terrible surprise when you think you're all set to graduate on time.

Participating in the advising available to you will maximize your chances of successfully passing your senior check, which is a system through which major advisors (again, folks like me) look at your record, check it against the requirements, read whatever notes previous advisors made on your file, and approve—or reject—your application for graduation. Yes, your application for graduation can be rejected. And it will be, if you haven't fulfilled the proper requirements for both your core curriculum (university-wide coursework) and your major. It happens; don't let it happen to you.

Participating in the advising available to you will maximize your chances of successfully passing your senior check

Once you've applied for graduation and passed your senior check, there's the usual stuff to deal with. Your college should give you a checklist (usually emailed directly to you with the notification that, yes, they're going to allow you to graduate, which is usually most student's first dawning realization that this was ever actually in question). You can use that checklist to make sure you meet the various deadlines. You have to inform the school whether you'll participate in the graduation ceremony, of course, and then buy your cap and tassel and rent your gown (usually—this can vary from school to school, but you always buy the cap and tassel). You can send out announcements, have pictures taken to commemorate the occasion, buy a class ring if you want. (You'll also get your first contact from your school's alumni association, which will be a consistent relationship you'll have with your alma mater whether you want it or not—seriously, these people will know you've moved before half your family and friends do.) But your next main event in the process—and also your last main event for your bachelor's experience in college—is commencement.

A couple of ironies about commencement: First, you'll be walking before final grades for that last term have been posted. So it's technically possible (though hopefully unlikely) that you could fail a course that you need to graduate, and be walking to receive a diploma that you can't actually have yet. And speaking of diplomas—that's the second irony. That piece of paper that they'll hand you at commencement doesn't actually have your diploma in there (partially because they know final grades haven't yet been posted). You'll get that in the mail a few months later . . . at least once you've settled all the bills you may still owe the university, from back-tuition to campus parking tickets.

To be perfectly honest, you may not actually *want* to walk through commencement once you get to that point in your college experience. A lot of students don't. By the time you're graduating, you'll probably be tired of all things collegiate. You will have just ended final exams for your senior year (and if you think that you had senioritis back in high school, wait for college) and, frankly, you're going to be tired. The ceremony is long, and you'd rather hang out with your friends (many of whom you may be saying goodbye to) and sleep in on the Saturday morning in May (or December) that your school schedules commencement for. But let's face it: You'll probably do it, maybe not for you, but for your folks. Or your grandparents. Or to inspire your younger siblings. Or for your whole family, because you're the first to graduate from college, or just because they love you and they want to recognize this huge thing that you've just accomplished—that they've probably helped you accomplish in different ways. And it is huge. And it does deserve recognition. A little pomp and circumstance, if you will.

To be perfectly honest, you may not actually want to walk through commencement once you get to that point in your college experience.

So slap a smile on your face, and walk. In a lot of ways, it's the culmination of all the work you've done—not only over the past four or so years in college, but for the 13-odd years (some of them extremely odd, especially in middle school) of your educational life before that. So put up with the picture posing, accept all the hugs and handshakes with grace, and live it up a little. You deserve it. After all, just like when you were a toddler . . . learning to walk opens up whole new worlds for you. So long as you remember to pay those student parking tickets first.

Sandra Mizumoto Posey

28. What You'll Need to Know from Day One of College to Get into Grad School

Advice from a Professor and Administrator . . .

Getting into grad school isn't all about grades and test scores (GRE, GMAT, LSAT, MCAT, LOLCAT, etc.).

Sure, that's part of it. You want to have a solid transcript that shows you took classes relevant to your graduate curriculum and that you did well in them. You want to study for those godforsaken tests and get a score high enough to qualify you for the institution you choose. But here's the real secret: A lot of getting into grad school (and getting funding for grad school) depends on your letters of recommendation.

Letters of recommendation for graduate school are generally from your professors, so make a point to get to know them and make sure they know who you are. If they don't know who you are, they **may** write you a letter of recommendation based on your grade in the class alone, but it will suck. It will say nothing remotely personal about you and your potential and that blah-ness will shine through loud and clear to whoever is on the other end reading it.

A good way to get your professor to know who you are is to participate in class and sit in the front. Don't be the annoying student who comments on everything and goes on and on without ever listening to anyone else or noticing that even their professor has mentally checked out during their diatribe. When the professor asks for participation, volunteer frequently but not every single time. Have your comments and questions be thoughtful, demonstrating that you wish to dig deeper into the material.

Performance in class hopefully isn't the only barometer by which your professor will measure you. Come by during office hours. This is a sure way to get noticed because, honestly, no one comes to office hours. We often use that time for other things because there is no one outside the door. Come by, show an interest in the class, and we'll love you. Even if what you have to say is that you are having difficulty with the material, we'll be impressed that you came for guidance and perceive you as a potentially stellar student.

If you have a professor who seems to recognize your potential or who is in the field you wish to enter, either take more classes from that professor or continue to visit them occasionally during office hours. Don't be a stalker, but come by to let them know you enjoyed their class and talk to them about their field of study. Ask them for advice. Professors love giving advice. After all, very few people actually pay attention to them.

When you're ready to apply for graduate programs, ask your professors what programs they would recommend. Often they will either recommend a place they themselves went to or a program where they have colleagues and friends they respect. A letter of recommendation from someone the committee personally knows will have a lot more weight than one from a professor the committee is not familiar with.

When you're ready to apply for graduate programs, ask your professors what programs they would recommend.

Finally, don't rule out grad school because it costs money and you're already in debt. Here's the secret: If you go into a field that is reputed not to make money when you come out of grad school, grad school is often free. There are fellowships, teaching assistantships, graduate assistantships, and various other ways to pay for grad school as you go. If, on the other hand, you're going into a field reputed to make money (say medicine or law for example), grad school will cost you but you'll presumably be making enough later to cover the payments.

By the way, if you do all of these things, you'll also get better grades, and that will also help you get into graduate school. You may also make a future friend and colleague. Believe it or not, professors have real lives and like getting to know you. That doesn't mean you should make a pass at them. Eww. That's a sure way not to get into graduate school. Or maybe to get laid if your professor is unethical, but then double eww.

Bridgette Coble

29. Get a Job! No, Scratch That. Get a Career!

Advice from a Director of Career Services . . .

You don't go to college in order to just get a job. We're not talking about the cashier gig you had at Burger King or the grocery store cart collector part-time shifts you worked after school and on the weekends.

When you make the decision to go to college, part of that decision includes preparing yourself for a career. A career gives you more than a paycheck. It encompasses more of who you are and becomes a part of your identity as a college-educated professional. Yes, I said it . . . *professional.* (Pretty word, isn't it?) That's what you can become after completing your college degree. But the path to becoming a professional is filled with challenges and requires you to do some work. Getting a college degree is one thing; becoming a professional is another thing entirely.

So why would you want to become a professional? It may remind you of the stiff-lipped, boring, poorly dressed adults you avoided as a child. The good news is you can be any kind of professional you choose. You can be hip, classy, trendy, elegant, glamorous, earthy, adventurous, or straight-up corporate. It's up to you. And that's the beauty of choosing a career. It's all about you. Think about the things you like, the kind of person that you are, the places where you feel most comfortable, the kind of people you want to be around. This will give you a clue to the kind of career professional you could be. Here's an exercise that can help: Close your eyes and picture yourself as a professional. What do you look like? What are you wearing? Where do you live? How do you get to work? Where do you work? What are you doing while at work? Do you take a lunch break? Do you eat out a lot? Are you in an office building? Are you working outside? Do you travel? The answers to these questions will give you some insight into your career direction.

OK, so now you might have an idea of the kind of professional you want to be. As a college student you will select a major. The major you choose will help you learn about a particular area of study and help you develop skills for the future. It can be helpful to choose a major that will help you as a career professional. For example, if you picture yourself as a politician, you might choose a major that helps you learn more about government, history, laws, and society. This would be a great start toward building a career in politics. It is important to think about how your major will help with your career, but it is not the most important factor. Your college degree is just one part of the decision. How you choose to spend your time as a college student is another important consideration.

Going to class, dating, studying, parties, dating, tailgating, and football games . . . did I mention dating? This is how we often think college students are spending their time. While this is true for most, there is another very important way students should be spending their time. Getting involved on campus is key to developing skills and making important connections that will help prepare you for your career. You might be asking, "What? Isn't it enough that I'm going to college?" No. Becoming a career professional starts with going to college and choosing a major, but you must also get involved and develop leadership skills. Think about it: Say a company has a job opening and wants to hire a new college graduate. They receive 100 résumés from students who are all completing a bachelor's degree. How are they going to select just one student? I'll tell you how: They'll look at the other things the student did while in school. They might look for students who were strong leaders on their campus or who worked for the school newspaper. They might want a student who has had some additional training through seminars or workshops. They might also care about students who gave back to their communities or learned how to work well with groups. Whatever it is, it will be a unique skill or characteristic or credit that goes above and beyond the degree.

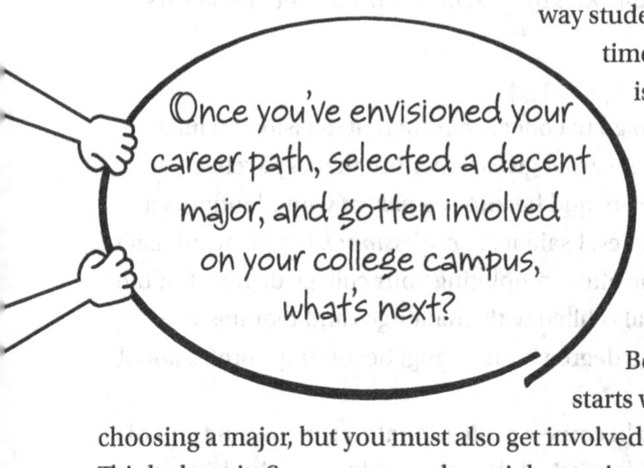
Once you've envisioned your career path, selected a decent major, and gotten involved on your college campus, what's next?

Once you've envisioned your career path, selected a decent major, and gotten involved on your college campus, what's next? Do career opportunities come knocking? Will an employer show up at my doorstep like Publisher's

Clearing House, smiling from ear to ear while presenting an amazing job offer and signing bonus? Dare to dream . . . but no, that's not how it's going to happen. You still have more work to do. This is the time where you begin to develop your professional image. Time to put away the sweatpants and jeans, take the metal out of your head, and hide the tattoos. Invest in professional appearance. You know: pressed shirts with collars, polished shoes, a haircut that costs more than a sandwich. (Quick tip: While you do have to invest some cash in this, it doesn't have to be high-cost—you can often find great professional stuff at thrift stores, so long as you're sure it looks professional now, and not back in 1987.) This is also the time to invest in a solid résumé. There are a lot of good places to discover this information (and not just elsewhere in this text): most campuses have career centers where they offer advice and even résumé checks to help students start on the right editorial foot.

So . . . got your degree? Check. Professional clothing? Check. High quality résumé? Check. General idea of the kind of career you want? Check. So now it's time to start networking, sending out résumés, and letting everyone know about your vision. Shake hands, kiss babies, make yourself known. The key to finding a career opportunity is knowing where to look, and knowing *how* to look. Don't just post your résumé on Monster.com, or rely on the contacts you've made on LinkedIn, or email companies that you're interested in working for—do all these things and more!

Remember that finding a career isn't rocket science—it's social science. Employers hire talented people who they genuinely like. You are talented and likable. You are talented and likeable. You are talented and likeable. (This is your new mantra.)

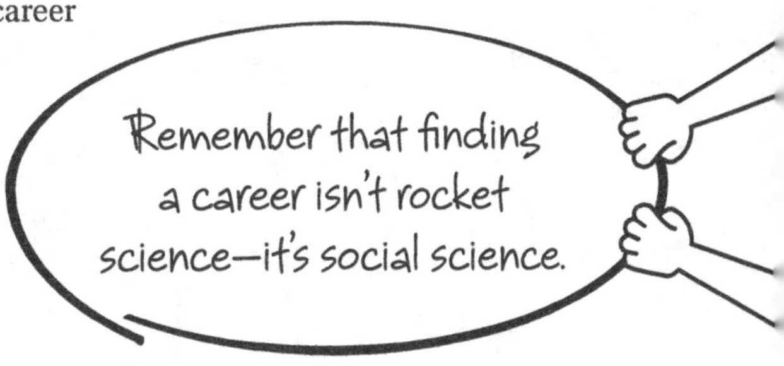
Remember that finding a career isn't rocket science—it's social science.

Now, go out and get that career!

section four

Student Perspectives

Andrewgenn/Fotolia

Daniel Alvarez

30. Picking a Major (Without Kicking Yourself Later)

Advice from a Student...

Sometimes I wish I could go back and kick my friends' butts. The truth is that I always had a pretty good idea of what I wanted to major in once I started college; it was my friends who thought my choice lacked, shall we say . . . practicality.

English had been my favorite subject since my freshman year in high school. I was that kid who had a backpack full of books that was so heavy that I almost dislocated my shoulder every time I picked it up. I was that guy whose phone rang every time one of my friends didn't understand the reading assignment for the next day. I knew all of Dante's circles of hell (and could tell you which circle you'd land in if you happened to die in a compromising position). I could explain how the bird was a metaphor in *To Kill A Mockingbird* and detail how Hawthorne's *Scarlet Letter* isn't about sex, even though it's about adultery. My friends depended on me like I was a walking Wikipedia of English lit. And even though they teased me for it, they also loved me for it. I'd even daresay that they admired me for it.

As graduation approached and college was around the corner, it came time to think about declaring a major. Clearly, there was only one choice for me. My love of literature, combined with all the time I had invested in the subject—tutoring friends, writing papers, cherishing the written word and all it can do—it was all leading up to one singular purpose in college. I chose—that's right—Accounting.

Allow me to explain.

Since I had been so generous in helping my friends out in high school, they collectively decided that college was where they would return the favor. Each of them had chosen a different focus in the exciting world of Business

Administration. So when they approached me with the question of what I was planning on majoring in and I proudly proclaimed that I'd be embracing English, the responses went something like this:

"English? What will you do with that?"

"What kind of job will you find . . . if you are able to find a job at all?"

And, finally, the most important question of all:

"How much money to do you expect to make with a degree like that?"

My first response was defensive. I mean, whose decision was this, anyway? It was mine. When I envisioned my college career, I pictured a time of fun and excitement. A place where I would get to study whatever I wanted to. English. Books. I would learn so much more about novels and their authors, about the art of writing. It would be the most glorious chapter of my educational career, and I couldn't wait.

But friends—especially at that age—can have more influence than they probably should. I gave in to what they'd suggested (and to be fair, they really thought they were helping me out), and enrolled in the Business College. I spent three semesters there, mostly dozing off in class and finding myself writing short stories in the margins of the 10-pound accounting text books I had to carry. It didn't just take its toll on me and my attitude—it actually made me give up. I left college feeling defeated and angry. The college experience had failed me, and it left me worse off than I was when I got there.

Leaving college after a year and a half led me not to re-embrace my love for English, but to believe that I had no other option but to dive into a career in retail. Instead of being a slave to business school textbooks, I became a slave to the customer. *"How much is this?" "Do you have this in a large?"* and *"Can I speak to your manager?"* became the new phrases du jour, and there was nothing I could do but grin and bear it . . . and eventually realize that this wasn't where I wanted to be either.

I haven't regretted a moment of the choice I made when I returned to college on my own terms.

So, finally, I made it back to school. This time, I chose the major that I wanted rather than the one that others thought was best for me and my economic future. I majored in English, and after a few years, I graduated with my bachelor's degree. And even then, I hadn't had my fill. I immediately enrolled in graduate school. I still don't know what specifically I want to do with my degree—or degrees. I still don't know how I'm going to make a living, or how big that living will be. But I do know this: I haven't regretted a moment of the choice I made when I returned to college on my own terms.

The truth of the matter is this: No one can tell you what the best path is, because it's different for everyone. The important thing to remember is that you are the only person who knows exactly what is going to make you happy. If you want to major in something that might not promise you a future of fame and fortune, go for it. Happiness is fortune in and of itself, and it lasts a lot longer than cash ever will.

This is college; it's time meant to explore, time meant to make the mistakes you won't be able to make once it's over and you're out in the "real world." You have to experience the whole gamut of it. Join clubs, make friends, and get involved in everything you possibly can. You never know where you'll find your passion.

Most importantly, whatever you do, don't let anyone get in the way of your dreams. Because who knows, you just might be end up like me, graduating years after you had expected to, waking up in the middle of the night because of a dream you were having where you lined up all your friends and one by one gave them a swift boot to the kadoot, and just before you kicked the last one you wake up because you realize you've been laughing out loud in your sleep.

Most importantly, whatever you do, don't let anyone get in the way of your dreams.

Believe me—it's much better than kicking yourself.

Megan Fowler

31. Tasting the Rainbow, One Friend at a Time

Advice from a Student...

You may think you know how to talk to gay people. But you don't.

At least most people don't, even those who consider themselves "enlightened" or support gay marriage on Facebook. This is one of the first lessons I learned when I came to college. One of the next lessons I learned was that I am a gay (I say *queer*) person myself. So it's my hope that I can spare you some of the embarrassment of my first experiences interacting with the GLBTQ community, and to make an easier time for everyone, including people like me. And people like you too.

The best advice for becoming an ally to these communities is to learn about them on your own. It is easier to demand to be educated by members of these communities themselves, but sometimes it's nice to not have people all around you chasing you down for fun facts about your identity and existence. Can you imagine if at every turn some person was asking you to recite the history of straight people? Or to draw them a blueprint of just how exactly straight sex works? There are people in positions to answer these questions for you; in fact, you pay them to do so, and they're called teachers. Unless you want to give a queer person a buck fifty for every tidbit of knowledge about their lives and preferences and likes and dislikes, I suggest you go the cheaper route of googling it. I have to admit that this is a lot of extra work, to learn a history for people your high school teachers probably pretended never existed, but it is important to understanding GLBTQ identities in order to understand why they need allies in the first place. Let me start you off with some free help: GLBTQ stands for Gay, Lesbian, Bisexual, Transgender, and Queer. (Start your search engines! 3! 2! 1! Google!)

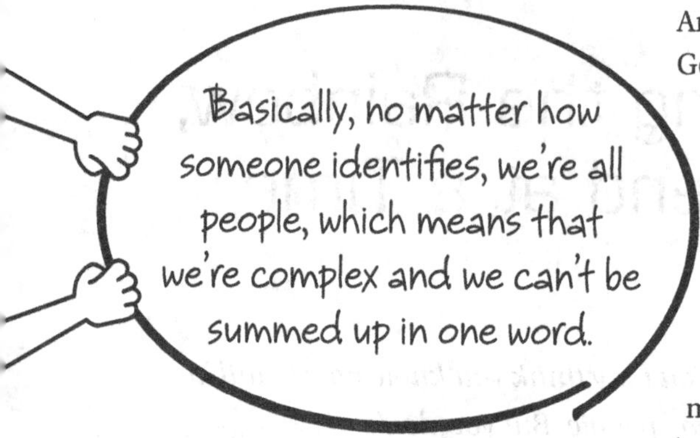
Basically, no matter how someone identifies, we're all people, which means that we're complex and we can't be summed up in one word.

Are you back? Have you googled? Good. I'm taking your word for it. My next piece of advice is perhaps the most important, so listen up! Queer people, straight people, trans people, gay people—the keyword here is *people.* Got it, people? Basically, no matter how someone identifies, we're all people, which means that we're complex and we can't be summed up in one word. In fact, people are like a googolhedron when it comes to sides of our personalities. Basically, we have a lot of sides to us and they all work together to make us unique little snowflakes. Just like being straight or cisgender (that means your birth sex, male/female, matches your gender, masculine/feminine)—you *are* these identities, but that isn't *all* you are. You might also be a student, a fan of rock and roll, a pessimist, a cowboy, and so on. Focusing on one of these identities and ignoring the fact that you are anything other than straight or gay makes people feel bad and erases their individualities. This is important, because all queer people are not the same. We don't all like pop music, fashion, or salads. Lesbians are not all hairy. Not all gay men like to go shopping.

One of the most wonderful things I've found in queer communities is a love for breaking the rules. It isn't that everything you know is wrong, so much as everything you know can be challenged if you have an open mind. In this case, having an open mind means challenging the rules of traditional attraction. One of the biggest stereotypes we have in our Western culture is that people are attracted to either men or women and that people are straight or gay. This is not the case. There are all kinds of in-betweeners out there who also need allies. Lots and lots of people are attracted to men, to women, to transgender people, to people of all genders. It is a mistake to think that bisexuals, pansexuals, or queer-identified people are in denial. That we need get over this "phase". Bisexuality is not a joke or a matter of indecisiveness; it's an identity, and it should be respected as one. As a future ally to GLBTQ communities, you'll have to open yourself up to all the colors of the rainbow.

Armed with your new knowledge, you may want to seek out queer people to enrich your life. But where should you look? Lucky for us all, queer people are just about everywhere. We're in your classes, in your dorm, probably even in your hometown. We shop at your grocery store, check out books at the library, and eat in the cafeteria. The problem becomes, how does one recognize these queer people? Unfortunately, physical appearance won't be too much help here. The "lesbian" pixie cut of yesteryear has entered the mainstream and those who still use that as a beacon of potential queer friendship might be disappointed when discovering that the owner of said hair is as straight as you are. Instead of these archaic methods, I would suggest getting involved with your campus Gay Straight Alliance if you are lucky enough to have one. If you don't, try volunteering at organizations in the community dedicated to GLBTQ rights. (Not only will you surely meet people from these communities, but it will also look great on a résumé.)

Once you've found your new queer best friends, make sure you remember that they're still people. They're not accessories for you. It's just not polite to show off your new queer friends to your other friends like a pair of new pumps. (Keep in mind that it's also unfair for the queer people in your life to treat *you* this way. You're not just a "fag hag," but a friend.) Don't be afraid to call people out if they're making you feel like an object.

The main thing you'll need to remember, no matter what community you might be meeting for the first time (that you know of) on a college campus—it's OK to make mistakes. It's OK to not know what you're doing. It's OK to have your pride hurt. As long as you learn from your mistakes—and you feel comfortable holding others honestly responsible for the mistakes that they make—then you'll know how to talk to gay people. Or, as they're also called . . . just *people*.

Adam Steininger

32. Roommates

The World Is Not Your Toilet

Advice from a Student . . .

Before your parents dump you off at college, they'll probably tell you something like "the world is your oyster." But I'd like to amend that idea. My words of wisdom for you are "the world is your toilet."

Or it can be if you let it be.

See, I used to have a roommate that thought the world was his toilet. (This is a common mistake for the below-average college student, since a two dimensional picture of Earth does look like a blue urinal cake.) Long story short, he came in from yet another in a long string of drunken late-nights, and mistook the middle of our dorm room floor for the commode. To put it bluntly, he peed all over the place. It was a good thing that we didn't have a rug. Or a dog.

And this isn't an accidental metaphor: As a college student new to dorm life, you may well have to metaphorically flush down your massive turd of a roommate, often without a proper plunger.

It wasn't that this roomie of mine was a bad guy. We were poorly matched, but that sort of thing is normal for dorm-mates—they don't pair you up based on personality tests, or shared hobbies, or anything approaching thought-out philosophy. (And even if they did, or your school does—and if they do, thank them for at least trying—the chances of you being besties with an assigned roommate are next to nil. Do you like everyone with whom you take classes within your major? Just because you're alike in one way means nothing to how dissimilar you may be in other, very important, ways. Like urination selection sites.)

Even in the best of cases, experiencing dorm life for the first time can be a tad unnerving. If you've never slept in the same room with someone for a year, you're in for a rude awakening. Living conditions in college dorms are poor, bleak, and full of bizarre-yet-vivid characters. Sort of like a Dickens novel, complete with the gruel (if you count ramen noodles). Another Dickensian similarity: Two people sharing a small space can have your room smelling and looking like an orphanage from the 1800s in no time.

There are no good answers to sharing a room with someone. Strangers are a complete crapshoot (sometimes literally, if you're as unlucky as I was) and rooming with friends carries its own problems. They say that you should never choose to live with a friend who you want to keep, and that's probably true. Living with someone who you love is tough enough (look at the divorce rate, or daytime TV, for proof of that); living with someone who you occasionally enjoy kicking back with is probably inviting trouble. You'll end up with a broken friendship to go along with your broken lease agreement.

The only things that you can do in working to create a better roommate situation are those things that you can control: namely, yourself and your behavior. In a roommate situation, you will get exactly what you give, eventually. If you're messy—if you leave chip bags and Starbucks cups everywhere, if you never empty the trash can, if you refuse to wash your sheets for an entire semester, then you're not only someone else's nightmare roomie, but you're going to get the same complete lack of care from them. (Maybe you're cool with smelly sheets and garbage everywhere—but consider the deodorant rule: You're not wearing Right Guard for you—you're wearing it for everyone who has to be around you.)

In a roommate situation, you will get exactly what you give, eventually.

So consideration is key. You'll still have arguments, because that's just how it works when two people are thrown into a small living space. (Try not to think about all the similarities dorm life has to prison. Trust me, you'll sleep better.) But if you have respect for the person you're rooming with, and if you refuse to treat the world like your toilet, you have a chance at enjoying the living conditions, and maybe coming out of the situation with someone you'll honestly want to keep in touch with over the years.

At the very least, I beseech you: Know where the bathroom is.

Thorin Klosowski

33. Why Taking Erotic Notes Is the Best Way to Remember Everything

William Taft on his sweet sixteen in a bathtub cursing corporations; 65 naked women petting 14 cats on the porch; Judge Dredd spanking Fred Sanford. When you need to remember facts, tidbits, or trivia for class, the best way to do it to tie them to weird and (potentially) erotic images.

Why? Because that's what your brain would rather think about right now.

Unless you have a photographic memory, one of the hardest tasks throughout your college career is to remember specific facts and pieces of information for classes you don't care about. Simply put, you don't care when William Taft signed the 16th Amendment, who betrayed Othello, or when the Renaissance took place. That's OK; you don't need those facts for the rest of your life, but you do need to remember them long enough to pass the next test. To do that, you need to make those facts important to you. If you're anything like I was in college, that means giving them an erotic touch.

To memorize anything, you need to tie it to something that matters to you. For me that meant combining lurid images with mundane details. If I need to quote Shakespeare, I'll put the line in the mouth of bikini-clad Audrey Hepburn while she rides a flying walrus. If I need to remember the years of the Renaissance, I'll tie it to a massive orgy. It's a basic mnemonic strategy to tie useless information to something that's important. When the information gets a little long winded—say, a bunch of facts for a test—then it's time to turn to a mnemonic device called the "memory palace," developed by the ancient Romans and Greeks to help visualize memories.

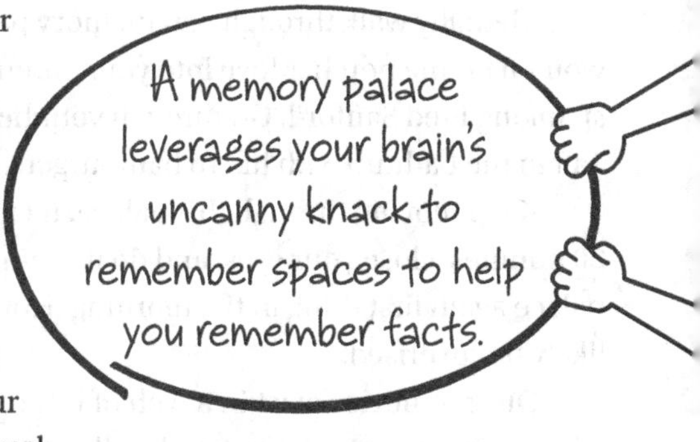

A memory palace leverages your brain's uncanny knack to remember spaces to help you remember facts. It's an ancient mnemonic device that attaches facts to a spatial location so you can easily remember them. It's very simple to build your memory palace: Start by taking a place you know very well—say, your childhood home. Mentally walk through the house, from the entrance, through the living room, on to your room, to the kitchen, and so on. You probably remember it surprisingly well, right? That's your first memory palace. Now it's time to fill that palace with the information you need to remember.

Let's say you're taking a U.S. history test on the amendments. For example, the 13th Amendment outlawed slavery and was adopted in 1865. How are you going to remember that? First, let's make a lewd image: 65 naked coeds (for 1865) petting 13 free-roaming cats (you can trade out cats for whatever animal you think of when you think of slavery). Now put that scene on the porch of your home: 65 naked women petting 13 free-roaming cats on the porch. That image is tough to forget, right? Now, let's move onto another amendment.

The 14th Amendment came out of the ruling in the Supreme Court case *Dredd Scott versus Sandford.* It gave slaves (and anyone else born in the United States) citizenship. What can we do with that? Let's put the comic book character Judge Dredd in your parent's room spanking Fred Sanford (of *Sanford and Son*) while a crowd of citizens cheers them on. Chances are you can't forget that image, and it's pieced together with everything you need to remember the 14th Amendment.

Walk through your memory palace again, starting with the naked women on the porch with the cats, and back into the room with Judge Dredd and Fred Sanford. Let's move on to the 16th Amendment. (Put the 15th somewhere in your parents' closet, just so you don't forget it.)

The 16th Amendment is easy. It was passed in 1913, mostly with the help of President William Howard Taft. It essentially added a special tax for corporations. So, what do we do with this? We connect all this information with history's funniest image—William Howard Taft (the most overweight of the presidents) in the bathtub, cursing corporations. Let's make him huge: say, 1300 pounds (for 1913), and surround him with 16 Big Macs.

Mentally walk through you memory palace again. Pass by the 65 naked women on the porch. Move into your parents' room where you left Judge Dredd spanking Fred Sanford. Go through your house until you see the 1300-pound Taft in the bathtub with his 16 hamburgers.

Keep moving through this palace, reciting what you see in each room. Wait 20 minutes, close your eyes, and do it again. Sleep on it and walk through the palace again first thing in the morning. How much do you remember? You'll likely be surprised.

Our memories exist in a web of interconnected facts. We remember what matters to us. We remember the strange. We remember the lewd. In your college years, when your brain is filled to the brim with sex, the easiest way to tie this all together is with the lewdest, nastiest things you can think of. The nastier the better, and the more likely it is you'll commit it to memory for the long term—or at least long enough to pass the test.

Our memories exist in a web of interconnected facts.

Finally, one last rule: Under no circumstance should you tell anyone the weird crap you think of in order to make this mnemonic magic happen. People will think you're as weird as you're thinking I am right now. But it works. That's what matters.

Jef Otte

34. Snark and Consequences

Lessons a Protest Taught Me

Probably the crowning achievement of my college career was that I once inspired a protest. With, like, picket signs and chants and everything. About a hundred people showed up, and they hated *me.*

It was glorious.

I was working for my college paper, which was completely run by students. The April Fool's Day issue was our Holy Grail. It was like smarty-pants Christmas. Traditionally, the issue was filled with fake news intended to fool the reader into thinking it was real, but we were generally less interested in fooling people than in being intellectually sarcastic. So that year, as the date approached, we decided we would do fake news, yes, but fake like *The Onion*—obviously fake. We would do satire.

Of course, satire is not always obvious. In fact, satire's most seminal work made waves chiefly because people missed the joke. You may have heard of it: Jonathan Swift's 1729 essay "A Modest Proposal for Preventing the Children of Poor People from Being a Burden to Their Parents or Country, and for Making Them Beneficial to the Publick," which suggested that the grotesquely impoverished Irish make a living selling the meat of their children to their rich English overlords—you know, in a funny way.

Many a monocle shattered that day.

These days, of course, we all share a hearty chuckle, because we're in on the joke: Swift effectively skewered English colonialism by exposing its hypocrisy, both in the work itself and in the English reaction to it. Genius.

Our goals were slightly less lofty. For my part, I wrote a column entitled "Enjoy obamacare if you like payin for illegal mexicans," an incoherent, badly punctuated screed about everything Republicans hate, written in the style of insane Tea-Party Internet commenters. The joke was partially that my column was regularly devoted to making fun of Republicans (yes, I admit it: I was a college liberal). Like Swift, though, I was also trying to make fun of stupid ideas by making them look stupid.

Unfortunately—despite that "A Modest Proposal" is widely taught at universities everywhere—my student colleagues largely took it literally.

Of course, it would be easy to take it literally if you were not familiar with either the paper or the column, which hardly anyone on campus was, because hardly anyone read it (which is why we got away with being student-run in the first place). And so on that fateful day, someone randomly picked up a copy and was shocked, *shocked*, by what they read. Word spread. By the time I rolled into campus all blissfully unaware of the controversy, I had already been widely denounced as a defamer and a racist, a protest was in the works, and a group of students had organized to remove all the papers from their bins around campus, so that the people protesting what I had written were unable to actually read it. It was a full-blown fiasco.

What else could I do? I showed up to the protest.

It did not go well. I was invited to speak on my own behalf and then got immediately booed off stage. The administration went into damage-control mode, issuing statements and holding panels with names like "Defamation in Satire versus Freedom of Speech" (actual name of a panel—it's also a fallacy, because satire and defamation are mutually exclusive in this case). But I did learn some important lessons.

The first I sort of already knew, but hadn't fully grasped: that words have power and, like Spider Man's uncle says, with great power comes great responsibility. Otherwise there are consequences and then you have no choice but to dedicate your life to fighting crime just to deal with the crushing guilt of your uncle's death. Or something like that.

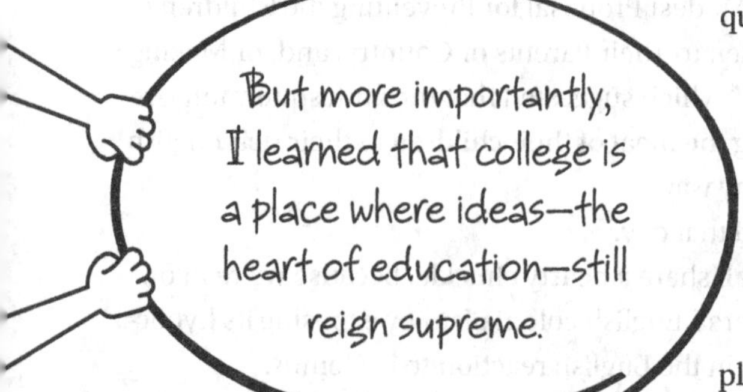
But more importantly, I learned that college is a place where ideas—the heart of education—still reign supreme.

But more importantly, I learned that college is a place where ideas—the heart of education—still reign supreme.

After all, I'd legitimately upset a lot of people. But—and this is a big BUT—no matter how mad I made anyone, and no matter how many problems I subsequently caused for the administration, nothing really happened. I didn't get kicked out of school. I didn't get fired. I didn't even have to stop being an editor. I graduated a month later with highest honors. Try finding a job where you tick off the bosses and then they have to reward you for it. That job does not exist. Well, maybe in unions.

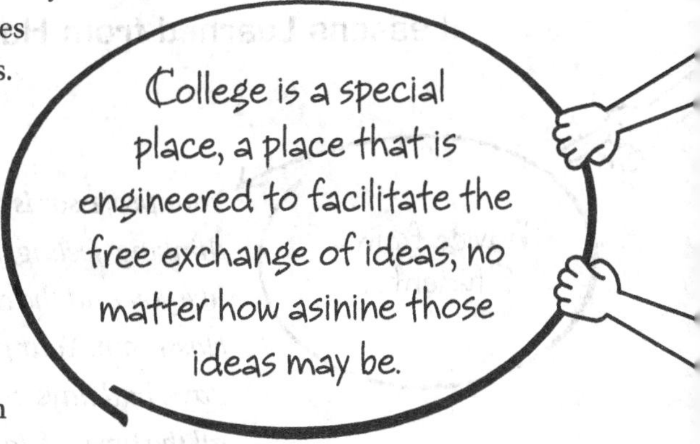
College is a special place, a place that is engineered to facilitate the free exchange of ideas, no matter how asinine those ideas may be.

College is a special place, a place that is engineered to facilitate the free exchange of ideas, no matter how asinine those ideas may be. People may not like them—a *lot* of people may not like them, even in the institution itself—but the institution is still structured to allow, protect, and even encourage that exchange—just like America. All you have to do is follow your interests as far as you want to go. Let me just repeat that: As long as you're interested, *you can do whatever you want.* And be rewarded for it!

Let freedom ring.

Tasha Ringo

35. The Truth about Your Professor

Lessons Learned from Hard Experience

Your professor is a living, breathing, thinking, feeling, judging human being just like you and the rest of the people in the classroom. Your professor will have good days, bad days, tired days, annoyed days... all the types of days you will have too.

So when dealing with your all-so-human professor, take a lesson from the first week of kindergarten: Not everyone will be your friend. And everyone includes the professor.

Your professor is not perfect. Your professor is an employee of the university who does not live in the office, sleep under the desk, or bathe and brush in the department bathrooms. (Even if you happen to see shampoo and toothpaste in there, don't assume.) Your professor has a home, maybe a family, maybe just a cat named Mr. Muffins. Your professor has a life, possibly friends, and likely plays drinking games while grading your midterm.

Your professor will not necessarily be fair. In the classroom you may feel offended, picked on, ignored, and subjectively graded because of the cut and color of your shirt on test day. You will be called on whether or not you raise your hand. When you want to speak the most, you will be passed by in the discussion. You will fulfill all requirements on the syllabus and still be marked down for not going above and beyond.

Your professor doesn't want to hear about it. Go ahead and sit down to discuss the unfair treatment you received. Politely explain to your professor that you were sick, sleep deprived (this excuse is especially ineffective), or that you feel very, very strongly about your opinion. Try to reason, come to an agreement, or see eye to eye. You will only irk your professor, further risking your final grade.

Your professor is part of the class. Be it biology, literature, computer science, statistics, or forensic accounting, you will have to study the professor too. You will need to learn the way the professor teaches. You will need to figure out the answers your professor wants to hear and see. You will need to discover what comments and opinions are acceptable to share with the class. You will have to study the professor in order to pass.

Your professor is in charge. If you want things to work in your favor, you will comply and do the work. The classroom is not a place to fight your personal vendetta or prove how awesome you think you are. The classroom is where you learn to pass the tests and attempt to stroke the pen that writes your grade.

Your professor has a boss. When you absolutely need to whine, there is a department chair, a dean, or even an advisor you can forward your complaints to. This is best done both after the semester is over and after you have exhausted your therapist's patience with the issue. When the real rules are broken, there is always someone to turn to: someone who is not your professor.

Your professor can be swayed. Remember those lessons from the first week of kindergarten, and play nice. Everyone enjoys a compliment on their shoes or accessories. Everyone likes to be heard and respected regardless of mutual opinions. Everyone enjoys a piece of chocolate before the final. (Just remember to bring enough for the whole class.) And everyone includes the professor.

Gellilla Gebre-Michael

36. Make Sure They Have Backpacks (and Other Rules for Surviving Freshman Year)

OK, I'll admit it: My Freshman year terrified me.

I wasn't going to my dream school, even though they'd offered me a small scholarship, because, well, it was too small, and I still couldn't afford it. Add to that disappointment the usual stuff about getting used to a new school—making friends, finding your way around, learning to be independent—it's easy to see how it can be the best of times and the worst of times. So you have to have some guidelines to follow, right?

Make Sure They Have Backpacks

The biggest obstacle I struggled with socially in my freshman year was determining who actually, you know, went to school there . . . as opposed to who was just there to pick up girls. Believe me, this really happens. After I unwisely gave my number to three different guys who turned out not to be the fellow students I expected, I started to realize—they didn't have backpacks. This was a sign. So when the next gentleman asked for my number, I asked him which school he went to. When he told me, I then asked him where the central building was for this school, which any student would have known. He pointed at a random building that was definitely not it. He was obviously lying—I was never so angry in my life! Be forewarned—these guys are out there. Some say that they're on campus just to hang out on their "days off" . . . when they don't actually have a job. Some will actually admit that they're there to score some "educated girls." (This was not the wording he actually used—he was a lot more graphic—but this is a family essay.) Here's the thing: You'll meet a lot of scrubs in your life, and college is too short to spend time on guys who lie to you about something so basic.

Leave Peer Pressure Behind

Everyone thinks that peer pressure is a high-school thing and that it disappears in college. It doesn't—your peers just change. It never really hit me how easily influenced I still was by my peers until after my freshman year was over. The number of times I skipped class to hang out with my friends simply amazes me now. The only way I realized how much I was messing up was because of my First Year Success instructor, who pulled me aside and asked if everything was OK because I had been missing class and just didn't seem focused. The fact that my teacher had noticed, before my so-called friends did, made me realize I came to school for a reason. I was here not only to get an education but to make decisions for myself. The people who can give a distinct reason of why they are going to school are the ones I finally realized I needed to surround myself with. College can either make you or break you. Work to let it make you.

Everyone thinks that peer pressure is a high-school thing and that it disappears in college. It doesn't.

Wait Until the Third Class

Gradually, I've become better at communicating with my teachers. The first couple of classes are always the most awkward because you don't want to look like an eager beaver, nor do you want to look like a slacker who will sit in the back of the classroom, not participate, and stay on Facebook the entire time. Take it from me; introduce yourself the *third* class period. The first day of class, you're still situating yourself and are not quite sure if you want to drop the course yet. In the second class, you're still going over the syllabus and attendance, and the teacher is naturally struggling to remember everyone's names.

After the third class, where they swear to have all of the class's names down by the fourth class, MAKE YOUR MOVE! Say something witty. Say ANYTHING! Just make sure your professor remembers you because of something positive. By the fifth class period, you'll probably have inside jokes with your instructor. You're in like Flynn! Please keep in mind that your college professors are NOT like your high school teachers. Yes, they want you to succeed; but chances are, they won't reach out to you. You need to make the effort. They're not going to bite you. They actually enjoy speaking to you. And don't forget: You might need a letter of recommendation in the near future. Who would be better than a close faculty member you've kept in touch with? (I'm currently fist pumping at my own advice.) One last thing along these same lines; wait until your third class—maybe even fourth—before you decide to drop the class. You just don't know what the "real" class is until the second week or so.

Give Yourself Time

One of my biggest obstacles in my freshman year was how I managed my time. If you are as easily distracted as I am, you'll soon find out that asking a friend to change your password on all of your social media networks (Facebook, Twitter, Tumblr, etc.) is extremely effective. Around midterms and finals, I beg my sisters to change my passwords. A day later . . . I usually beg for it back! But you have to have control over yourself. Have faith. Once you get into the habit of managing your time wisely, you won't have to ask others for help. Now I manage my time by writing my weekly goals on a large whiteboard in my room. Keep in mind, it doesn't have to be on a whiteboard. It could be on sticky notes stuck to your bathroom mirror, a piece of paper on the fridge, or even daily reminders on your phone. With my whiteboard, it's the first thing I see before I even leave my room. If you think you won't commit to these tasks, tell a friend. Tell a family member. Hell, tell Facebook so that you're cyber friends can remind you. Just don't discourage yourself. You can do this!

One of my biggest obstacles in my freshman year was how I managed my time.

Are these the only tips you'll need for surviving freshman year? Not at all. But they're my top few, the things I needed to learn in order to make all the years that followed successful. Dream school or not, it's your education—keep your backpack with you at all times, and see how far you can go.

afterword

Sunscreen for the 21st Century

Andrewgenn/Fotolia

Back in the dark, dark times of the pre-millennium—namely the 1990s—there was this little thing that was starting to hit the mainstream. Maybe you've heard of it, because it did pretty well for itself: the Internet. Along with the Internet came a lot of other things: the ubiquity of email, spam as referent to something that isn't processed meat-stuffs, and the meme. You know, those little mini-fads that you hear about and then can't help but look up and enjoy yourself, so you can feel part of the cultural zeitgeist. Well, one of the first memes from the web was an urban legend (which later became a song and video directed by none other than Baz Luhrmann) called *Sunscreen*.

Sunscreen (or, if you're talking about the song, "Everybody's Free to Wear Sunscreen") was a litany of life lessons supposedly attributed to Kurt Vonnegut, who was said to have delivered it to the graduating class at MIT in 1997. But that's not who wrote it; nor did Vonnegut speak at the MIT graduation that year. It was actually a Chicago Tribune column written by Mary Schmich, who blamed the whole misunderstanding on the "lawless swamp of cyberspace."

In any case, it was meant as a sort of graduation speech—one that Mary Schmich said she would have given to the graduating class of that year, should she have been asked. And here's the thing: It's full of great advice, like "don't be reckless with other people's hearts, and don't put up with those who are reckless with yours," and "enjoy the power and beauty of your youth," and (of course): "floss."

So here's our own version of sunscreen, drawn from the individual pieces that we've set before you in this snarktastic book. Think of it as a reminder of all the stuff that we've talked about, and a quick-reference page for those pieces of advice that you might want to most recall moving forward in your lives, outside of college, diploma in hand, into the world that awaits.

Have a good life.

Foreword, Forewarned

- Who really reads instruction manuals? (page xii) You should. Take it in. Even those books that don't look like instruction manuals are, in fact, instruction manuals. And unlike the directions that come with that blender you just bought, most of life's instruction manuals—novels, nonfiction, the stories your grandparents tell—are actually pretty entertaining.

Before Class

- Toss out those security blankets; you don't need them. (page 2) You might always have things you cling to, but in this time of great change? Might as well rid yourself of all the silly things on which you may still be dependent.
- If you're smart, you'll communicate, collaborate, and commiserate at the appropriate times. (page 5) This is always true. In every situation. Smart people know when to do which, and then, you know, actually *do it*. Sometimes knowing you should do something feels like enough. It's not.

- Know what you know, and know what you don't know. (page 8) This is the Socratic ideal—knowing that you don't know is the first step to coming to know it. It's as true now as it was back in the days of rhetoric, public baths, and hemlock.
- Get out there and talk to people. (page 11) Talk to everyone you can. Do it humbly. Listen. Drink in the experiences of other people—especially people who are older than you. There's a reason that elders used to be the most respected members of a culture. It should still be that way, because they've been around.
- Know all the cool little stuff. (page 14) Sure, learning a trade is important. Working on the big problems in our world is also important. But knowing who won the World Series in 1952, who wrote *One Flew Over the Cuckoo's Nest,* and who sculpted *The Thinker*? These are worth knowing as well. (Just for the record: the New York Yankees, Ken Kesey, and Auguste Rodin.)
- You have enormous potential. (page 16) The only thing that ever limits what each individual is capable of is their own self-doubt. That sounds cosmic, but it's not. Just two hundred years ago, most of our light came from fire. Only a little over a century ago, man couldn't fly. A couple of decades back, hands-free telecommunication was still only on *Star Trek.* The things we see as impossible now are only things that we haven't figured out how to do yet.
- Make sure that the things you pay for with borrowed money are things you won't regret paying for later. (page 20) This is the goal. You'll fall short of this goal often. Aim for achieving this most of the time, and you'll be ahead of most American purchasers.
- Professors are there to help. (page 27) This should be self-evident, but based on the evidence from thousands of professors around the country and across the world, many students still don't get this.
- The only way to do it wrong is to stop working at it. (page 29) Work is the baseline for everything you do. Nothing that's worth anything comes easily, and there's value in sweat, literal or figurative.

In Class, with Class

- You define who you are and what you can do based on your work. (page 32) And this is why work is so important. Your work becomes who you are, who you present to the world. Whether that work is your career, or your passions, or your children, or your charitable contributions to a cause—that work is you, and how you shall be known.

- Never ask anyone what they are. (page 35) Really, it's just a rude question. Even if it's asked with the best of intentions, a rude question is still a rude question.
- If you don't understand something, ask questions. (page 39) Questions are how invention comes about, and invention is how we move forward as a society and as a people. Never let fear of the answer keep you from asking the question.
- Practice safe learning. (page 42) Practice safe everything, really. But don't make the mistake of confusing "safe" with "not scary." Bravery isn't not being afraid—it's being afraid of something and doing it anyway.
- Being interested makes you more interesting to others. (page 45) It also keeps you from being so self-involved that you become insufferable. So there's that.
- Refer to your goals to find out what's really important. (page 48) If you can see the endpoint, the path becomes clear. Eyes on the prize.
- Assume that someone is always watching. (page 51) We're all at our best when we think we're being monitored. Even if it's just you watching, someone's paying attention.
- College is in part about learning how to ask questions. (page 53) So is life in general, by the way. Never stop questioning.
- A few points are better than no points. (page 57) Like Wayne Gretzky said, "you miss 100% of the shots you never take." Take the shot.
- Sometimes that small change in grade makes all the difference in the world to a student's GPA. (page 59) Small changes always make big differences, or can. Margaret Mead's take on this idea was, "Never doubt that a small group of thoughtful, committed citizens can change the world; indeed, it's the only thing that ever has." Small pebble, big ripples.
- You write, you write, you write. (page 62) Everyone does. So why do so many students think they don't need to learn to write well? There isn't a job in the world that doesn't get easier, doesn't allow greater success, if you're a good writer.
- You're not as subtle as you think you are. (page 65) You're generally not as anything as you might think you are. In other words, don't get cocky, kid.

Beyond Class

- Sometimes putting all your eggs in one basket works. (page 71) And all those aphorisms you may have heard in your life? May not be completely true.
- Know that your next boss will Google you. (page 73) Welcome to life in the new millennium.
- It's hard to understand your culture until you see it from an outside perspective. (page 77) In other words, it sometimes takes leaving a place to understand what it's like to really be there.
- Slap a smile on your face and walk. (page 80) Good advice, just in general.
- Volunteer frequently, but not every single time. (page 83) Consider participation mandatory—including in working to meet your own goals.
- You are talented and likable. (page 85) You're good enough, you're smart enough, and doggone it, people like you.

Student Perspectives

- No one can tell you what the best path is. (page 90) Not even this text has all the answers.
- It's OK to make mistakes. (page 93) Everyone does. Learning from them is the trick.
- Know where the bathroom is. (page 96) Knowing the location of this, along with the closest available exit? Always a good idea.
- We remember the strange. (page 98) This is the guiding philosophy of this text.
- Words have power. (page 101) The power to persuade, the power to punish, the power to elevate. Words have toppled governments, ruined relationships, and formed bonds as strong as any emergency or action. There's a reason our leaders tend to be well spoken. Because words matter.
- Everyone enjoys a piece of chocolate. (page 104) Really, this is indisputable.
- See how far you can go. (page 106) Absolutely. Push it. Keep pushing. Write when you find work.